Victoria Sylvia Evans

Ladies-in-Waiting:
Women Who Served
at the Tudor Court

Introduction

Although a great deal of material has been published on Henry VIII's household and the organisation of the Tudor court as a whole, the role of women has been somewhat overlooked and even diminished. Some historians suggest that women's roles narrowed down to being mere ornaments of the court. While it is true that physical appearance played an important part in selecting women who served the Tudor queens, ladies-in-waiting were powerful figures in their own right and enjoyed positions of privilege at court. This book delves deep into the roles of ladies-in-waiting and maids of honour at the court of Henry VIII. Drawing on a variety of sixteenth-century sources, such as manuscripts, household lists, chronicles and personal letters, this author portrays a collective image of women who served at the Tudor court.

Part 1: Inside the Queen's chambers

Chapter 1:

Layout of a royal household

The Tudor court was the place to be for anyone who wanted to build a successful career, but not everyone could be described as a "courtier". The definition of a courtier narrows down to male and female aristocrats who were closely linked to the royal household and government. Gentlemen of the King's Privy Chamber and the Queen's ladies-in-waiting were part of the "above stairs" staff, known as *Domus Regie Magnificencie,* and thus were considered courtiers, while staff working "below stairs", the *Domus Providencie*, were responsible for the provisioning of the court, and servants working there were not described as courtiers.

While members of both above stairs and below stairs staff served the King, there was a significant difference between a lady of the Queen's Privy Chamber and a kitchen maid. The latter was considered a menial servant, while the post held by the former was considered to be a privilege and a mark of high social standing.

The court regularly moved between the royal palaces that lined the Thames—Greenwich, Whitehall, Hampton Court and Windsor were among the favourites—so that each residence could be cleaned and aired. Each summer, when the plague was often rife in the city of London, the royal entourage went on a royal progress, making a series of visits to aristocratic homes scattered around the countryside. In whichever residence the royal couple was staying, they required a suite of rooms known as the privy lodgings, where they would be secluded from the main court.

The set of rooms inhabited by the King, Queen and courtiers was divided into "outward" and "inward" rooms. The Great Hall—one of the most splendid examples still surviving at Hampton Court Palace—was a place were lower-ranking servants dined, lived and slept on a daily basis. It was also a stage for celebrations and great banquets. The more private set of rooms where the royals and aristocracy lived and conducted their business was known as the "inward" set of chambers, lined up one behind the other.

The King and Queen had separate households and thus separate sets of rooms, but the Queen's side was organised in such a manner as to mirror the King's. The Queen's suite was accessed through the Watching Chamber, leading to the Presence Chamber and into the Privy Chamber. Each room was guarded by servants of the crown who allowed fewer and fewer people to enter as they walked through.

Pedro de Gante, a Spaniard who came to England in the entourage of the Duke of Najera in 1542, recorded the progress of the duke's party "through three halls, hung with tapestry". In the Watching Chamber, he saw "the King's bodyguard, dressed in habits of red, and holding halberds". In the main ceremonial room of the court, the Presence Chamber, there were "nobles, knights, and gentlemen, and here was a canopy made of rich figured brocade, with a chair of the same material". The throne beneath a rich cloth of estate was a focal point of this room and denoted the monarch's continuous presence in the chamber. "To this canopy and chair the same respect was paid as if the King himself were present", the Spanish secretary observed, adding that everyone was standing on foot, their caps removed from their heads as a sign of respect.

The Presence Chamber served as a place where foreign visitors were entertained and here, "the brother of the Queen and other noblemen entertained the duke a quarter of an hour, until it was announced that he should enter the chamber of the King".[1] Pedro de Gante was not allowed to enter the King's Privy Chamber with his master and his closest companions; apparently, he wasn't important enough to see the King during a private audience. Pedro de Gante's account is particularly interesting because it gives us a rare glimpse

---

[1] *Narrative of the Visit of the Duke of Najera*, ed. Frederic Madden, p. 10.

into the Queen's side of the royal household. After an audience lasting half an hour, the Duke of Najera emerged from the King's Privy Chamber and was conducted to the "chamber of the Queen [Katherine Parr]" and led into her Presence Chamber where "stood another canopy of brocade, with the chair of the same".[2]

The Privy Chamber, where only a small group of trusted attendants or high-profile visitors was admitted, led directly to the bedchamber. Later in Henry VIII's reign, the bedchamber became a part of the Privy Chamber, comprised of a dressing room ("raying chamber") and a closet or stool chamber (the equivalent of a modern toilet). In the Privy Chamber, the Queen could relax surrounded by her most trusted attendants and hide from the prying eyes of other courtiers.

The number of women who served the Queen in her Privy Chamber remained steady throughout Henry VIII's reign. In 1509, Katherine of Aragon had thirty-three women serving her in the Privy Chamber, and Katherine Parr had the exact same number of female servants in 1547.[3] The competition for places was fierce, and women strived to forge individual relationships with each Tudor queen.

---

[2] Ibid., p. 11.
[3] Barbara J. Harris, *English Aristocratic Women*, p. 216.

Chapter 2:

Selecting the female attendants

Identifying the factors that determined the Queen's choice of her female attendants is not impossible, although due to the lack of formal documentation, it poses certain difficulties. Henry VIII was married six times in total but only two of his wives, Katherine of Aragon and Anne of Cleves, were foreign princesses of blood. The King's four remaining spouses were native Englishwomen who underwent a transition from maid of honour or lady-in-waiting to Queen consort, developing a new phenomenon at the Tudor court. Both Anne Boleyn and Jane Seymour were Katherine of Aragon's maids, while Katherine Howard served Anne of Cleves.

There is no concrete evidence that Katherine Parr served as lady-in-waiting to any of Henry VIII's wives because she lived mostly at her husband's estates, presiding over a vast household and supervising her stepchildren's education. She did, however, come to court in 1542, where she became Mary Tudor's lady-in-waiting and caught Henry VIII's eye. The experiences of these four women shed some light upon the qualities required of the ladies-in-waiting, and their households provide an extraordinary wealth of information about the structure and rotation of servants within their Privy Chamber.

It seems that it was the Queen and not her Lord Chamberlain who was responsible for selecting women to serve her, although in some circumstances the King interfered either on his own account or after being consulted.[1] In April 1533, for instance, he summoned Anne Bray Brooke, Baroness of Cobham, to attend Anne Boleyn's coronation as the attendant horsewoman. "We therefore desire and pray you, to put yourself in such a readiness, as you may be personally at our manor of Greenwich the Friday next before the said feast", the King ordered.[2]

In 1544, on the other hand, when Henry VIII was away on a war campaign in France, Katherine Parr wrote to him, asking to "know our pleasure for the accepting into your chamber of certain ladies in places of others that cannot well give their attendance by reason of sickness".[3] All of Henry VIII's subsequent queens drew heavily on their predecessor's staff; in consequence, many female servants smoothly passed from one royal establishment to the next.

---

[1] The Lord Chamberlain was nominally in charge of the Privy Chamber and supervised the staff.
[2] Henry Ellis, *Original Letters Illustrative of English History*, p. 275.
[3] Muriel St Clare Byrne, *The Letters of King Henry VIII*, p. 367.

In choosing their Privy Chamber staff, Tudor queens sought well-educated, good-looking and skilled aristocratic women. Instructions for Princess Mary's household of 1525, drawn by the King and his council, stipulated that ladies and gentlewomen serving within the royal household were obliged to "use themselves sadly, honourably, virtuously and discreetly in words, countenance, gesture, behaviour and deed with humility, reverence, lowliness due and requisite" and to avoid "evil or unfitting manners or conditions".[4] Similar guidelines concerning behaviour of candidates for the Queen's service were sent by John Husee to Honor Grenville Plantagenet, Lady Lisle, in 1537. Acting as the agent of the family at court, Husee wrote to the Lady Lisle cautioning her that "it shall please your ladyship to exhort them [her two daughters] to be sober, sad, wise and discreet and lowly above all things, and to be obedient, and governed and ruled by my lady of Rutland [Eleanor Paston Manners] and my lady of Sussex [Mary Arundell Radcliffe], and Mrs Margery [Horsman Lister] and such others as be your ladyship's friends here; and to serve God well and to be sober of tongue".[5]

Husee felt obliged to warn Lady Lisle that "the court is full of pride, envy, indignation, scorning and derision", and thus young ladies serving about the Queen were entering into

---

[4] J.L. McIntosh, *From Heads of Household to Heads of State*, p. 6.
[5] Elizabeth Norton, *Jane Seymour*, p. 133.

a dangerous place. In times when a woman's honour was highly prized, it was important to keep away from scandals, harmful gossip and licentiousness, not only for the sake of one's reputation but also, or maybe above all, for the sake of their family's honour, as Husee remarked in his letter.

Places in a royal household were much sought after by noble families, but it would be a mistake to assume that only one's noble origin ensured a place within the Queen's household. Each queen was free to appoint whomsoever she chose to her Privy Chamber, although each was obliged to respect family ties and remain loyal to their supporters.

When Katherine of Aragon's household was reorganised after Prince Arthur's death, she felt obliged to provide for her Spanish servants, treating them as if they were her family. Many of Katherine's Spanish ladies-in-waiting who stayed with her during the seven-year period of her penurious widowhood were rewarded with lucrative posts when Katherine became Queen in 1509.

Henry VIII married four of his female subjects, and they were obliged to provide for their families, bringing their favourite female relatives to court. Close relatives were not only placed close to the Queen out of family loyalty but often for the sense of security that such a post brought. Anne Boleyn, for instance, appointed her female relatives because she did not have a lot of supporters outside family circles. Katherine Parr, on the other hand, was tied to some influential noblewomen not only by blood but, above all, by faith.

Although positions surrounding the Queen were not hereditary, many women came from the families with a long tradition of service to the crown. Mothers of Henry VIII's English-born queens served as ladies-in-waiting to his first wife, Katherine of Aragon; for instance, Maud Green Parr, Katherine Parr's mother, enjoyed a close relationship with the Queen, who became her daughter's godmother. However, noble origin, family ties and religious common ground were not the only crucial factors in obtaining a place within the Queen's household. The political influence of their families and possession of necessary physical attributes, certain social accomplishments and womanly skills, such as sewing and embroidering, were equally important.

Language skills played an important role in selecting female attendants. The language of the cultured at court was French, and its importance was emphasized before Katherine of Aragon came to England in 1501. Although she was a royal princess, Katherine had not been taught French, her Spanish family having always been on bad terms with the French ruling dynasty. Queen Elizabeth of York, wife of Henry VII, and the King's mother, Margaret Beaufort, were concerned about Katherine's lack of training in foreign languages; she spoke only Spanish, which was barely spoken in England, and Latin. The two women advised the girl that she "should always speak French" with her sister-in-law "in order to learn the language, and to be able to converse in it when she comes to England." The Spanish ambassador concluded that "these ladies do not understand Latin and much less, Spanish".[6] With time, Katherine eventually managed to learn English as well, although in 1506, five years after her arrival in England, she begged her father to send her a Spanish confessor because "I do not understand the English language nor know how to speak it".[7]

To be able to speak French was a powerful recommendation; in 1518, when the Treaty of Universal Peace was nearing completion, a magnificent courtly pageant was organised to honour the French ambassadors. The gorgeously apparelled "lady maskers took each of them a French gentleman to dance and mask with them". It was noticed that "these lady maskers spoke good French, which delighted these gentlemen, to hear these ladies speak to them in their own tongue".[8]

The importance of language skills is well demonstrated by the experiences of Henry VIII's second wife, Anne Boleyn.

---

[6] *Calendar of State Papers, Spain*, Volume 1, note 203.
[7] David Starkey, *Six Wives*, p. 96.
[8] *Letters and Papers*, Volume 4, footnote 26.

When she became one of the Archduchess Margaret of Savoy's maids of honour, she was praised by her royal mistress for her proficiency in French as well as for the overall impression she made on her arrival to Brussels in 1513 at the age of twelve. In her letter to Anne's father, Thomas Boleyn, who had been an ambassador to Brussels at the time, the archduchess wrote:

"I have received your letter by the Esquire Bouton who has presented your daughter to me, who is very welcome, and I am confident of being able to deal with her in a way which will give you satisfaction, so that on your return the two of us will need no intermediary other than she. I find her so bright and pleasant for her young age that I am more beholden to you for sending her to me than you are to me."[9]

Anne's first independent letter written to her father from the archduchess's court clearly shows that she was well aware that mastering the French language was her main goal:

"Sir, I understand from your letter that you desire me to be a woman of good reputation when I come to court, and you tell me that the Queen will take the trouble to converse with me, and it gives me great joy to think of talking with such a wise and virtuous person. This will make me all the keener to persevere in speaking French well and also especially

---

[9] Eric Ives, *The Life and Death of Anne Boleyn*, p. 19.

because you have told me to, and have advised me for my own part to work at it as much as I can."[10]

There are even details of how Anne Boleyn was learning French under the tutelage of Symmonet, one of the teachers in the archduchess's household:

"Sir, I entreat you to excuse me if this letter is badly written: I can assure you the spelling proceeds entirely from my own head, while the other letters were the work of my hands alone; and Symmonet tells me he has left the letter to be composed by myself that nobody else may know what I am writing to you."[11]

When Henry VIII's younger sister Mary was preparing for her journey to France in 1514, where she was about to marry the King Louis XII, she specifically requested to have Anne Boleyn in her entourage, having probably heard about the girl's progress in the French language.[12] When Mary Tudor was widowed after three months of marriage to the ailing King, she hastily married Charles Brandon, Duke of Suffolk, and soon left France. Anne Boleyn, however, retained her position as maid of honour within the household of the new

---

[10] Ibid.

[11] Henry Ellis, *Original Letters Illustrative of English History*, pp. 11-12.

[12] Eric Ives, *The Life and Death of Anne Boleyn*, p. 27.

Queen of France, undoubtedly due to her excellent progress in French.

Upon her return to England in 1522, Anne Boleyn was "so graceful that you would never have taken her for an Englishwoman, but for a Frenchwoman born". She embraced not only the French language but also manners, fashions and culture, and soon became Katherine of Aragon's maid of honour, although we may assume that Katherine, who was never fond of the French, frowned upon Anne's Frenchness. It couldn't have been welcomed among the English courtiers who, only two years earlier, disparaged Henry VIII's minions who returned from France as "all French in eating, drinking and apparel, yea, and in French vices and brags".[13]

Anne Boleyn was credited with excellent knowledge of the French, being "very expert in the French tongue, exercising herself continually in reading the French Bible and other French books of like effect and conceived great pleasure in the same".[14] But when she fell out of favour in 1536, the King condemned her "French bringing up and manners".[15] Nevertheless, Anne Boleyn's continental education set her apart from other women at court and, although never

---

[13] Jessie Childs, *Henry VIII's Last Victim*, p. 80.
[14] Eric Ives, *The Life and Death of Anne Boleyn*, p. 268.
[15] *Calendar of State Papers, Spain*, Volume 5 Part 2, note 61.

considered to be a great beauty, she "excelled them all" in "behaviour, manners, attire and tongue".[16]

Not that much is known about Jane Seymour's language skills or her education in general. The nineteenth-century historian Agnes Strickland believed that Jane, like Anne Boleyn, spent some time in France, first as Mary Tudor's maid of honour and then transferred to Queen Claude's household. This claim arose after a portrait in the French collection was erroneously labelled as a full-length depiction of Jane Seymour in her early twenties.[17]

Jane's family was not as prominent at court as Anne's, but her elder brother Edward managed to carve out a successful career, and it was perhaps due to his intercession that Jane found a place as Katherine of Aragon's maid of honour.[18] In 1536, when Jane became Henry VIII's love interest, the imperial ambassador Eustace Chapuys observed that she had been long at court, suggesting a long-term courtly career rather than a recent arrival.[19]

---

[16] Eric Ives, *The Life and Death of Anne Boleyn*, p. 45.

[17] Agnes Strickland, *Memoirs of the Queens of Henry VIII*, p. 218.

[18] The imperial ambassador Chapuys wrote that Jane "was a maid of the late Queen, and afterwards of Anne Boleyn" (*Letters and Papers,* Volume 11, note 64)

[19] *Letters and Papers*, Volume 10, note 901.

Although she is generally dismissed as plain or uninteresting, Jane Seymour must have possessed a set of skills that made her a perfect candidate for a maid of honour. Perhaps it was her proficiency with the needle since she was considered an expert seamstress, and Katherine of Aragon's favourite pastime was needlework; the Queen may have been paying particular attention to young girls with a skill for needlecraft when seeking new female attendants.

When it comes to proficiency in foreign languages, the only indication of Jane Seymour's skills comes from the imperial ambassador Chapuys, who was invited to Jane's apartments to congratulate her on her marriage on 4 June 1536. Chapuys spoke in French, and Jane seemed to understand everything the ambassador said to her and replied to his overtures of friendship, promising to keep Lady Mary, Henry VIII's elder daughter, in the King's good graces and agreeing that she would do everything in her power to earn the name of the "preserver and guardian of peace" which Chapuys so kindly bestowed on her.[20]

Jane was able to talk to the ambassador without a translator, although after this short exchange of diplomatic niceties, the King, "who in the meantime had been talking with the ladies of the court", approached the two and "began

---

[20] *Calendar of State Papers, Spain*, Volume 5 Part 2, note 61.

making excuses for the Queen" saying that Chapuys "was the first ambassador to whom she had spoken; she was not used to that sort of reception".[21] From this, we may infer that Jane either showed signs of nervousness during her first diplomatic duty, or that she was doing rather well and the King did not want his wife to meddle into politics too much.

Katherine Howard, Henry VIII's fifth wife, was probably the least educated of Henry VIII's English wives, but she was very young when the King married her, and therefore she still had plenty of time for educational pursuits. Her only extant letter was written in the inexperienced hand of a love-stricken teenager, her style of writing not as elegant or elaborate as that of her cousin's, Anne Boleyn.

Katherine Parr, the King's sixth and final wife, acquired a reputation of a lady with scholarly interests. Katherine Parr's knowledge of the French language was very good since she learned it within her mother's household, but her Latin was rudimentary. Nevertheless, she embraced the opportunity of brushing up on the language when she became Queen and keenly embarked on studies to improve her knowledge of it. There is a possibility that Katherine knew Italian as well since she received a letter in this language from Henry VIII's younger daughter Elizabeth; it seems unlikely that Elizabeth

---

[21] Ibid.

would have written in Italian if she knew the Queen wouldn't be able to read it without the assistance of a translator.

The fact that neither Katherine Parr nor her sister Anne was proficient in Latin may suggest that young noblewomen were taught only a base familiarity with this language. Anne Boleyn used to lament her ignorance of Latin, but we may never know if she did so because she felt her Latin was rusty or because it was a "polite convention to plead inadequacy".[22]

Not all women who came to court were inexperienced when it came to service. The practice of sending gently born children into the service of their family's peers was well established throughout the Tudor period. Children growing up in such households were not servants per se but were always treated with the respect of their birthright and counted as part of the family. Apart from mastering foreign languages, they learned to take part in hunting, dancing and other amusements they would later exploit at court. Girls were taught the art of writing letters, attending the lady's toilette, sewing, embroidering and cooking, as well as managing the estates and supervising servants.

Katherine Parr's mother, who became a widow in 1517, created a household for young children of both sexes

---

[22] Eric Ives, *The Life and Death of Anne Boleyn*, p. 45.

within her own estates. One courtier opined that in Maud Parr's care, his grandson "might learn with her, as well as in any place that I know, as well nurture, as French and other language, which to me seems was a commodious thing for him".[23] The motto Katherine Parr adopted when she became Queen—"to be useful in all I do"—may well have been harking back to the education she received at her mother's side.

The competition for places within Tudor queens' households was fierce, although there was an element of choice because there were other royal establishments where women could seek employment: those of Henry VIII's sister Mary Tudor Brandon, his daughters Mary and Elizabeth, and later in his reign, Anne of Cleves, when she was proclaimed Henry VIII's "beloved Sister" and treated as such after the annulment of her marriage to the King.

Parents often played crucial roles in obtaining places for their daughters. Thomas Howard, Duke of Norfolk, secured a place within Anne Boleyn's household for his thirteen-year-old daughter Mary. As Anne's cousin, Mary Howard was admitted, although the minimum age for a maid of honour was sixteen. The fact that age was an important factor in securing a position for one's daughter within the Queen's household is proved by the experiences of Lady Lisle's daughters.

---

[23] David Starkey, *Six Wives*, p. 694.

At some point in May 1536, after having heard that her two nieces were appointed as Queen Jane Seymour's maids of honour, Lady Lisle decided to seek similar preferment for one of her daughters. Her choice fell upon the younger one, Anne Basset, who, by all accounts, was both good looking and intelligent. Anne's age, however, posed a certain problem because she was deemed "too young" to become the Queen's maid, being probably less than sixteen years old.[24]

Even the fact that Anne had previously spent three years in the household of a well-connected French noble family at Pont de Remy near Abbeville did not help her become the Queen's maid; indeed, it may have even been held against her. Queen Jane Seymour was determined to avoid everything French, including fashion and manners, to distance herself from her executed predecessor, Anne Boleyn.

Lady Lisle, however, did not give up on the idea of having her daughter in the Queen's service. She decided to change tactics and offer Katherine, her elder daughter who was of "sufficient age", instead of the younger Anne.[25] Unfortunately, the Queen had already appointed all of her female servants, and none of the Basset girls were admitted to the royal household at the time.

---

[24] Muriel St Clare Byrne, *The Lisle Letters: An Abridgement*, p. 202.
[25] Ibid., p. 203.

The only alternative to obtaining a position for one's relative at court was to place her in the service of one's peers. The Lisles' agent, John Husee, suggested that Katherine Basset should become Lady Sussex's servant in order to stay at court. Unfortunately, Lady Sussex already had several young girls under her wings and could not take Katherine, but Margery Horsman Lister agreed to take her if her husband would allow it.[26]

The perk of being a servant of the Queen's lady-in-waiting was to be in frequent attendance at court and to see the Queen on a daily basis; Margery promised to bring Katherine Basset "into the Queen's chamber every day". There was also a plan to situate Katherine in the Duchess of Suffolk's household. At seventeen, the duchess was about two years younger than Katherine Basset, but she was the wife of Henry VIII's loyal companion and friend, Charles Brandon, Duke of Suffolk, and thus a very influential noblewoman. Anne Basset, on the other hand, was about to become Lady Rutland's servant after the summer progress, "when all heats and dangers of sicknesses be past".[27]

Considering the fact that Henry VIII was rapidly changing wives in quick succession, the role of ladies-in-

---

[26] Ibid., p. 204.
[27] Ibid.

waiting and maids of honour as the Queen's advisers increased. Women, who acquired considerable experience serving at court for years, were an invaluable source of information on courtly ceremony and introduced each queen to their new responsibilities, helping them to carry out their new duties.[28] In turn, the queens often became susceptible to their servants' opinions, and these opinions often affected the recruitment of new members of the royal household.

In his letter to the Lady Lisle, John Husee reported that "my Lady of Rutland [Eleanor Paston Manners], at her coming to court, will be in hand with my Lady Beauchamp [Anne Stanhope Seymour] and other of her friends to help (if it be possible) that one of your daughters shall be immediately preferred unto the Queen's service at the next vacant, which is thought shall be shortly".[29] Queen Jane finally agreed to pick one of the girls when she was satisfied with the contingent of delicious "fat quails" shipped from Calais by the Lisle family.[30] Husee reported:

"Madam, upon Thursday last, the Queen being at dinner, my Lady Rutland and my Lady Sussex being waiters on Her Grace, Her Grace chanced, eating of the quails, to common [speak] of your ladyship and of your daughters; so that such

---

[28] Barbara J. Harris, *English Aristocratic Women*, p. 211.
[29] Muriel St Clare Byrne, *The Lisle Letters: An Abridgement*, p. 205.
[30] Ibid.

communication was uttered by the said two ladies that Her Grace made grant [promise] to have one of your daughters . . ."

However, the Queen was determined to "first see" the girls in order to "know their manners, fashions and conditions, and take which of them shall like Her Grace best".[31] Anne Basset seemed more agreeable to the Queen, and she was finally sworn in as her maid of honour on 15 September 1537, only one day before Jane Seymour "took to her chamber" for the ritual seclusion before birth.[32] Katherine Basset, who was not picked, settled for a position in Lady Rutland's service. The importance of intercession by the Queen's ladies was emphasized by John Husee, who asked Lady Lisle "to send thanks as well to my Lady Beauchamp as to my Lady Sussex and my Lady Rutland, for divers causes".[33]

Physical appearance played an important part in securing a position within the royal household, as women were expected to take part in revels and masks, and to entertain foreign guests and the royal couple with dances and singing, activities which played a central part of courtly life. One of Henry VIII's first recorded mistresses, Bessie Blount, was praised by a contemporary who wrote that "in singing,

---

[31] Ibid., p. 207.
[32] Ibid., p. 208.
[33] Ibid.

dancing, and all goodly pastimes, she excelled all others".[34] The King fancied himself as a poet and musician and apparently paid much attention to women with similar talents. Anne Boleyn, the woman who refused to become his mistress and captivated him for six years, was praised by contemporaries for her musical abilities; "she knew perfectly how to sing and dance . . . to play the lute and other instruments".[35] Katherine Howard, Henry's teenage fifth wife, was taught to play the lute and virginals when she was raised in the household of Agnes Tilney, the Dowager Duchess of Norfolk.

The importance of physical appearance in the ideal female servant was emphasised in 1500, when the Spanish ambassador reported that "the King and Queen [Henry VII and Elizabeth of York] wish very much that the ladies who are to accompany the Princess of Wales [Katherine of Aragon] should be of gentle birth and beautiful, or at least that none of them should be ugly."[36] It was a general opinion among ambassadors that the English people, especially the King, were "thinking so much as they do about personal appearance."[37]

---

[34] Barbara J. Harris, *English Aristocratic Women*, p. 221.
[35] Eric Ives, *The Life and Death of Anne Boleyn*, p. 29.
[36] *Calendar of State Papers, Spain*, Volume 1, note 268.
[37] *Calendar of State Papers, Spain*, Volume 1, note 419.

Anne Basset's appearance played a crucial part in her preferment to the Queen's Privy Chamber, which is attested by several contemporaries, including Henry VIII himself. On 7 October 1537, the King was talking about Lady Lisle and her children with his favourite courtiers and opined that Anne Basset was "the fairest".[38] He was obviously smitten with her since the family agent, John Husee, reported in December that "the King's Grace is good lord to Mistress Anne, and hath made her grant [promise] to have her place whensoever the time shall come."[39] Henry VIII was referring to his eventual remarriage since Queen Jane died on 24 October 1537, soon after giving birth to Prince Edward, ending Anne Basset's short career as maid of honour. The King kept his word, and Anne retained her post with his subsequent wives.

Apparently, she continued to enjoy influence with Henry VIII; in 1540, she interceded with him on behalf of her sister Katherine, who was still unsuccessfully trying to be admitted to the Queen's household. The King, however, refused to appoint Katherine, saying that he "would have them that should be fair, and as he thought meet for the room [suitable for the post]".[40] From this we may infer that Katherine Basset was not as good looking as her younger

---

[38] Muriel St Clare Byrne, *The Lisle Letters: An Abridgement*, p. 211.
[39] Ibid.
[40] Barbara J. Harris, *English Aristocratic Women*, p.221.

sister Anne. In fact, it seems that two of Lady Lisle's four daughters, Anne and Mary Basset, were exceptionally good looking. Their physique played a crucial role in planning their futures: although Lady Lisle had two elder daughters, Katherine and Philippa, aged between sixteen and eighteen, she had chosen her youngest daughters, Anne and Mary, aged between twelve and thirteen, to be educated with the French noble family.

In a letter to Lady Lisle, Madame de Riou, who took Anne Basset under her roof, wrote that Anne was "esteemed very fair and of good conditions" by everyone who met her.[41] Madame de Bours, who took Mary Basset, praised her appearance, saying that "she is beloved of all them that see her . . . it makes me not a little proud that they should say she is fairer than Mistress Anne".[42] In his letter to Lord Lisle, Madame de Riou's husband wrote that "as for Mistress Marie, who is with my sister [Madame de Bours], she is merry, and is indeed the fairest maiden in the world to look upon".[43]

Similar sentiments were expressed by Peter Mewtas, Gentleman of the King's Privy Chamber, who, upon hearing that Henry VIII "thought Mistress Anne Basset to be the fairest", told him that Lady Lisle's "youngest [Mary Basset]

---

[41] Muriel St Clare Byrne, *The Lisle Letters: An Abridgement*, p. 116.
[42] Ibid., p. 114.
[43] Ibid., p. 115.

was fairer".[44] It seems that Lady Lisle's decision to send Anne and Mary Basset to be educated in the French noble households was motivated by the girls' apparent good looks and charm, coupled with their mother's hopes for the future; they were raised and trained to become the Queen's servants and secure better marriages than their elder, less attractive, sisters.

Interestingly, none of Henry VIII's English-born wives were considered beautiful at the time. Anne Boleyn was only "reasonably good looking", according to her cleric, but nevertheless managed to capture the King's attention. Her complexion was not fashionably pale but swarthy, covered with "small moles incident to the clearest complexions".[45] She was "of middling stature" with "bosom not much raised" and long neck. She wore her dark hair loose on occasions, threaded through with diamonds, rubies and pearls. All contemporaries agreed that Anne's long hair and "black and beautiful" eyes were her strongest features.[46]

Hostile sources would later exaggerate her imperfections, claiming that she had a sixth finger on her right hand, while she only had "a little show of a nail" on one of her fingers. She was also ascribed with a hideous swelling under

---

[44] Ibid., p. 211.
[45] Eric Ives, *The Life and Death of Anne Boleyn*, p. 40.
[46] Ibid., pp. 40-41.

her chin and a projecting tooth. If Anne Boleyn indeed had such glaring physical imperfections, she would never have been admitted to the Queen's household since it was generally believed that a hideous appearance only mirrored one's sinful soul. Anne was "not one of the handsomest women in the world" but was good looking enough to become Katherine of Aragon's maid of honour and attract the King's attention.[47]

Jane Seymour, Anne Boleyn's successor, was "no great beauty", and the only thing in her physique worth praising, according to her contemporaries, was her pale complexion. The imperial ambassador reported that she was "so fair that one would call her rather pale than otherwise".[48] When the King wanted to remarry after Jane's death and fell in love with a portrait of Christina, Duchess of Milan, the girl's skin tone was compared to Jane Seymour's; "she is not so pure white as the late Queen, whose soul God pardon, but she hath a singular good countenance".[49] Henry VIII's fifth wife, Katherine Howard, was described as a lady of "moderate beauty, but of very attractive deportment, little and strong, of modest

---

[47] Ibid.

[48] *Letters and Papers*, Volume 10, note 901.

[49] *Letters and Papers*, Volume 12 Part 2, 1188.

demeanour and mild countenance".[50] Katherine Parr, praised for her sense of style, had "a lively and pleasing appearance".[51]

Impeccable manners and good education, pleasing physical appearance and accomplishments in at least one sphere—whether in music, needlework or any other—were crucial in selecting female attendants for the Queen. But despite their talents and accomplishments, the main reason for women's presence at court was to serve the Queen and carry out their duties as well as they could.

---

[50] *The British Critic and Quarterly Theological Review, Vol.21, F. and C. Rivington, 1837,* p. 298.
[51] Pedro de Gante, *Narrative of the Visit of the Duke of Najera*, p.12.

Chapter 3:

Organising the women according to their rank

There were three essential groups of women serving in the Queen's household. Ladies-in-waiting, known also as Ladies of the Privy Chamber, attended to the Queen's daily needs such as washing, dressing and serving at the table. Chamberers performed more menial tasks such as arranging bed linen and cleaning the Queen's private chambers. Maids of honour attended the Queen in public, carried her long train and entertained her with singing, dancing or reading poetry or books aloud.

Maids of honour were unmarried girls of at least sixteen years of age, although sometimes they were younger. They were usually daughters or close relatives of influential courtiers of high social status. To ensure their seemly behaviour, the young maids of honour were supervised by the "Mother of Maids". During the reigns of Henry VIII's daughters, Mary and Elizabeth, the post of maid of honour evolved into Maid of the Privy Chamber, and the number of such servants was much higher than during the reign of Henry VIII.

Queen Elizabeth I never married, and some young women followed in the Queen's footsteps and voluntarily shunned matrimony, growing old at court. Such women were advanced from the posts of maids of honour to Gentlewomen of the Privy Chamber, a post normally reserved for married women. This phenomenon was aimed at rewarding the women who could or would not marry for the years of their devoted service in Queen Elizabeth's Privy Chamber.[1]

Ladies-in-waiting were married women of high rank. A small number of them were connected to the Queen's Privy Chamber solely by virtue of their husbands' posts, but most of them held their positions due to their own experience and talents. A suitable marriage was a qualification needed in order to progress from a position of maid of honour to lady-in-waiting, and the example of Mary Howard, Duchess of Richmond, best illustrates such an advancement; she was Anne Boleyn's maid of honour and became her lady-in-waiting when she married the King's son. Later, Mary Howard became the "extraordinary" member in the household of Henry VIII's sixth wife, Katherine Parr.

---

[1] Charlotte Isabelle Merton, *The Women Who Served Queen Mary and Queen Elizabeth*, p. 41.

"Extraordinary" membership[2] in the Privy Chamber was reserved for women of high social status who were either very wealthy and in no need of direct payment or had their own vast households to supervise and could not serve in the Queen's household on a daily basis. These women were summoned to court for special occasions such as banquets, coronations, christenings or the reception of foreign ambassadors.

Anne Boleyn's step-grandmother, the Dowager Duchess of Norfolk, carried her train during her coronation procession but was not a regular member of Anne's household because she was running a household of her own where she trained aristocratic but impoverished young women, including Henry VIII's fifth wife, Katherine Howard, to enter society upon their maturity. Anne of Cleves, who became Henry VIII's "beloved Sister" after the annulment of her marriage, was summoned to court during festivities and other grand events and listed as the "extraordinary" attendant of Katherine Parr in 1546.[3] The "ordinary" members, on the other hand, were those ladies of the Privy Chamber who served the Queen constantly, attending to her everyday requirements.

There were also other women who served the Queen but fell outside the Privy Chamber organisation. They were the

---

[2] The extraordinary ladies were also known as the great ladies.
[3] *Letters and Papers*, Volume 21 Part 1, note 969.

Queen's female fool and laundress. The fool was permitted familiarities without regard for deference and drew the Queen's attention to delicate matters in the form of a joke. According to one contemporary account, Anne Boleyn's female fool had been to Jerusalem and spoke several languages. When she saw that her royal mistress was not honoured by the citizens of London during her coronation procession—they did not greet her with the customary "God save the Queen" or take their caps off when Anne passed by—she retorted that they were keeping their caps on to cover their scurvy heads.[4] The laundresses were not of high birth and usually served for long periods of time. When Katherine of Aragon arrived in England with her entourage in 1501, she brought her personal laundress with her, as did Anne of Cleves in 1539.

---

[4] *Letters and Papers,* Volume 6, note 585.

Oath

Upon entering service in the Queen's household, women took the ceremonial oath, forging a bond of mutual obligation between them and their royal mistress. The servants were obliged to render their service loyally and obey the Queen in everything. The oath was usually witnessed by senior staff members if women were joining the Queen's household after it was first formed. The oath's power to create political allegiance is illustrated by the example of Katherine of Aragon's long-term servants who refused to call her Princess Dowager or to leave her service when in 1533 the Archbishop of Canterbury proclaimed that her marriage to the King was invalid. One of the King's servants, Thomas Bedyll, reported that:

"All women, priests and ministers of the Princess's [Dowager] chamber, as sewers, ushers and such other, who fetch any manner of service for her, call her the same in the name of the Queen, for she has commanded them. They all consider that they ought to call her Queen still, considering that those who appertain to the chamber were sworn to King Henry and Queen Katherine".[5]

A dispute arose between Henry VIII and Katherine of Aragon and her old servants. The King was desperate to move

---

[5] *Letters and Papers,* Volume 6, note 1253.

on and start a new life without Katherine as his wife, but Katherine's resolve did not weaken even after the Archbishop of Canterbury proclaimed her marriage to Henry VIII invalid. Believing that, as the anointed Queen of England and Henry VIII's true wife, she could not be cast aside, Katherine refused to acknowledge her new position declared by the King. Even Anne Boleyn's coronation in June 1533 did not change Katherine's attitude towards this matter. Having no other option left, on 5 July 1533, the King issued a proclamation confirming that his marriage to Katherine of Aragon was invalid, and anyone who would insist on calling her "Queen of England" instead of "Princess Dowager of Wales" would "clearly and manifestly incur . . . great pains and penalties" specified in the said declaration.[6]

Although all of the Queen's servants were swearing their loyalty to her, they owed a dual loyalty: one to Henry VIII as their sovereign and the other to the Queen as the head of her household. Although the oath taken by the Queen's servants is not extant, it is discernible in *The Instruction Book* issued for Princess Mary's 1525 Welsh household. The wording of her councillors' oath makes it clear that they owed loyalty to the King as much as they did to the Princess:

---

[6] Patrick Williams, *Katherine of Aragon*, p. 344.

"You shall be a true and faithful servant unto the King our Sovereign lord Henry the eighth and unto his heirs . . . And you shall be faithful and true unto my lady Princess Grace . . ."[7]

However, not only the servants had certain obligations towards their Queen. She, in turn, was obliged to provide for them because they depended on her for their livelihood, room and board. Katherine of Aragon, for instance, felt a strong sense of commitment towards her servants, especially towards the women who followed her into exile. On 7 January 1536, as she lay dying at Kimbolton Castle, Katherine implored Henry VIII to pay marriage portions to her three remaining ladies.

Household regulations

Once sworn in as ladies-in-waiting or maids of honour, women were expected to obey the household regulations. The 1540 ordinances of the Queen's household stated that the head officers were tasked to read the household regulations before all the servants so that they were well acquainted with their duties.[8] Stealing goods or disrupting the order within the household was forbidden and punished adequately. The first

---

[7] J.I. McIntosh, *From Heads of Household to Heads of State*, Chapter 2, p. 2.
[8] B.L., Harleian MS 6807, f. 10v.

violation of a household ordinance carried a warning, but a second transgression brought an instant dismissal from the royal service. The Queen's servants were advised not to be "pickers of quarrels or sowers of discord and sedition" and warned neither to "fight nor brawl nor give occasion to do so".[9] All of the servants, including women, were to keep silence inside the Queen's chambers as well as during mealtimes in the Great Hall.[10]

Wages and livery

The Queen's servants were to be dressed "cleanly and decently", and they received livery which signalled the membership to her household.[11] Materials used for livery gowns for the female servants throughout the entire reign of Henry VIII were usually damasks, velvets and satins. Many of the liveries were russet in colour. Katherine of Aragon's female servants, especially her chamberers, were periodically provided with liveries. On 18 October 1511, four chamberers—Elizabeth Collins, Elizabeth Lisle, Margaret Pennington and Elizabeth Vargas—received gowns of damask furred with miniver. Three years later, a similar order was

---

[9] B.L., Harleian MS 6807, f. 11.
[10] Ibid.
[11] B.L., Harleian MSS 6807, f. 12.

made for Elizabeth Collins, Blanche Merbury, Margaret Mulshoo and Elizabeth Vargas. They were supplied with russet damask for gowns. Women usually received materials for their liveries rather than already made gowns, and they hired tailors to make them up in whatever designs were fashionable at the time.

Liveries could be used to express powerful political statements. In December 1530, when the proceedings to secure the annulment of Henry VIII's marriage to Katherine of Aragon dragged on, Anne Boleyn commanded her servants' liveries to be embroidered with a defiant motto, "Ainsi sera, groigne qui groigne", which means, "What will be, will be, grumble who may". This was Anne's declaration against her enemies because, although she was treated with utmost respect and reverence by Henry VIII and his close friends, the French ambassador observed that "the people always remain hardened against her and . . . they would do more than they do if they had more power".[12] Anne's provocative new livery did not last long, however. She discontinued it as soon as she learned that she had adopted the motto of the imperialists, her bitter enemies.[13]

Katherine of Aragon was no less provocative when in July 1533 she ordered a brand new livery for her servants. It

---

[12] *Letters and Papers*, Volume 4, note 5016.
[13] Paul Friedmann, *Anne Boleyn*, p. 128.

was embroidered with the intertwined letters "H" and "K" standing for "Henry" and "Katherine", as though they were still a married couple.[14]

Jane Seymour provided "nothing more but wages and livery" for her maids of honour, and paid them £10 a year.[15] She also made it clear that each should have one servant to wait upon them and that they should provide their own bedding.

All women who served at court had to be apparelled "according to their degrees", but instead of denoting their social standing, clothes denoted their position in the household. The Queen's maid of honour, for instance, wore more sumptuous gowns than a servant of a duchess or countess.[16] The maids were also entitled to draw materials by warrant from the Great Wardrobe for feasts such as Christmas and Whitsun.

Jane Seymour was very particular about the clothes worn by her attendants and required that the newly appointed Anne Basset should wear out her French wardrobe and obtain an English gable hood, which, according to John Husee, "became her nothing so well as the French hood". Jane

---

[14] *Calendar of State Papers, Venice*, Volume 4, note 923.
[15] Muriel St Clare Byrne, *The Lisle Letters*, Vol. 4, p. 191.
[16] Ibid., p. 166.

Seymour also required a new "bonnet of velvet and frontlet of the same" for Anne, and John Husee opined that the girl's mother could lend her some of her own "old apparel", which "would serve this matter for Mrs Anne . . . for a time".[17]

From this, we may infer that Jane Seymour did not grant daily attire to her female servants. Upon her arrival at court, Jane Seymour's experienced lady-in-waiting, the Countess of Sussex, provided Anne Basset with a kirtle of crimson damask and matching sleeves. The Queen, now confined to her private chambers and awaiting the birth of her first child, changed her mind and decided that Anne "shall wear no more her French apparel" and should be provided with "a gown of black satin, and another of velvet" before the churching ceremony. Even Anne Basset's smocks and sleeves were faulty since they were "too coarse".[18]

The birth of Prince Edward on 12 October 1537 generated a set of new requirements for Anne Basset's clothing. She was ordered to have "a new gown of lion tawny velvet, or else one of black velvet turned up with yellow satin" for the Prince's christening (she was hastily provided with the latter) and a new "satin gown" to wear at the Queen's churching ceremony. The approaching Christmas festivities

---

[17] Ibid., p. 164.
[18] *Letters and Papers*, Volume 12 Part 2, note 808.

required a brand new gown "of lion tawny velvet". All gowns had to meet the standards in Mrs Pole's "book of reckoning".[19]

Jane Seymour's death twelve days after her son's birth did not put an end to the clothing requirements. Anne Basset needed no new gowns until her "mourning gear be cast off", although she needed "a new gown of lion tawny satin" for Christmas because it was uncertain "how long the King's pleasure should be that they [the Queen's ladies] should wear black". The new gown had to be provided just in case he changed his mind.[20]

Not much is known of the livery of Anne of Cleves's servants. She came to England apparelled in the fashion of her country, and her servants wore their own distinctive apparel and were criticized for their heavy dresses and headgears. Katherine Howard returned to the French fashion and expected her ladies do the same. Fancy hats gained popularity toward the end of Henry VIII's reign, and thus Katherine Parr's ladies wore her badge pinned to their caps. All of Katherine Parr's servants were regularly provided with black livery, the same as Henry VIII was providing for the Gentlemen of the Privy Chamber at the time.

---

[19] Ibid., note 923.
[20] Ibid., note 1157.

Livelihood, room and board

There were many privileges women of the Privy Chamber could enjoy. Serving the Queen provided ample opportunities to access the monarchical ear and obtain certain favours when royal support was vital for the successful outcome of petitions or legal suits. Apart from being close to the royal mistress, however, there were other privileges such as regular salary, board and accommodation.

Luckily, we have one very significant piece of information on how courtiers were rewarded for their service. In 1526, Cardinal Wolsey issued the Eltham Ordinances, which laid down instructions aimed at making life at court more ordered. One of the most important perquisites was receiving the "bouche of court"—the right to receive food, drink and day-to-day materials—written down in a document stating precisely what each person should receive according to their rank. A maid of honour, for example, received:

". . . one chett lofe [brown loaf], one manchet [small white loaf], one gallon of ale; for the afternoon, one manchet, one gallon of ale; for after supper, one chett lofe, one manchet, two gallons of ale, dim pitcher of wine; and from the last day of October unto the first day of April, three lynckes [torches], by the week, by the day, six sises [small candles], one pound of white lights, six talshides [timber for fuel], six faggots".[21]

Ladies-in-waiting were not listed as one cohesive group. Instead, there were regulations touching duchesses, countesses, baronesses and knights' wives who served in this capacity.[22] Apart from the "bouche of court", the Queen's ladies-in-waiting and maids of honour received room and stabling for their horses. Because they were themselves of high social rank, they were entitled to bring their own servants to court. The Eltham Ordinances were particular about how many servants and horses the Queen's ladies were permitted to keep. Among the highest ranking noblewomen were dowager duchesses who were allowed to stable twenty horses and lodge seven servants.

In many instances, the number of horses and servants permitted depended on whether or not a noblewoman's husband was lodged at court; a countess who was a widow or whose husband was out of court could stable fourteen horses and keep four servants, but a married countess living with her spouse at court was allowed to stable eight horses and keep two servants.[23] It was forbidden to overreach the assigned

---

[21] Society of Antiquaries of London, *A Collection of Ordinances and Regulations*, p. 164.
[22] Ibid., p. 165.
[23] Ibid., p. 199.

number of horses and servants, although the rules were broken on many occasions.

Chapter 4:
Daily Routine

It is difficult, although not impossible, to reconstruct a "typical" day for any of the six wives of Henry VIII or their female staff. There were many demands on the Queen's time: religious observances, domestic matters to be acted upon, charitable enterprises and receiving foreign ambassadors. Here, we shall follow the Tudor queens and their court through a typical day at one of the royal residences, and we shall imagine that it was not a particular feast day, but a day without any specific duties to attend or foreign ambassadors to be received, a day like any other.

The Queen would wake up in her luxurious four-poster bed, with its hangings often made of cloth of gold or crimson satin and adorned with an embroidered coat of arms emphasizing her lineage. The earliest risers were the Queen's closest attendants. The Eltham Ordinances of 1526 minutely listed the duties of the King's gentlemen, ushers, and grooms of the Privy Chamber but did not do so in the case of the Queen's maids of honour, ladies-in-waiting and chamberers. However, since the Queen's household mirrored that of the King's, we may assume that the female staff performed some of the functions of the men in the King's Privy Chamber, although it is difficult to draw definite conclusions about their positions.

When Anne Basset was admitted as one of Jane Seymour's maids of honour, John Husee wrote to her mother that Anne "furnisheth the room of a yeoman usher", and some historians since have suggested that she would have had the same responsibilities as the King's yeoman ushers, including guarding the entrance to the Privy Chamber and preparing the suite in the morning. Some, however, doubt that since the detailed lists of Katherine of Aragon's and Anne of Cleves's households listed male yeomen ushers.

We will assume that male yeoman ushers were tasked to prepare the Queen's suite of rooms in the morning, as described in the Eltham Ordinances. They were expected to be up and about at seven o'clock in the morning, or earlier, if they received direct instructions from the Queen the night before. Two yeomen ushers would start their guard at the Privy Chamber's door by eight o'clock and see that only the right people were admitted, and they gave the orders for the grooms and pages. The grooms were bound to appear in the Privy Chamber between six and seven o'clock in the morning to clean the Privy Chamber, light fires, carry torches and lights and fill the space with the pleasant scent of herbs to disguise any foul smells spilling from corridors or kitchens. The Eltham

Ordinances emphasised that the royal suite of rooms should be "dressed, repaired and made clean and good order of service and attendance used in the same."[1]

We do not know when each of Henry VIII's wives woke up; Henry VIII himself was an early riser, especially when he was in the prime of his youth, and rose daily at 4:00 or 5:00 a.m. to indulge in his favourite pastimes, such as hunting and hawking, leaving the matters of state to the likes of Cardinal Wolsey. One of the King's personal servants would often be found sleeping in the same bedchamber on a pallet bed if the King was spending the night without the Queen.

We may assume that the Queen would similarly have one of her female servants sleeping in her bedchamber as well. We know that Henry VIII's daughter Mary was busy from the earliest hours, but Elizabeth admitted that she was not "a morning woman" and was absent for most of her Privy Council's meetings.[2] Sadly, there is no information about the rising hours of Henry VIII's wives in the primary sources. We may assume that straight after awakening, the Queen would wash her face and hands in a basin of water. There is no evidence that any of Henry VIII's wives used the luxurious

---

[1] Society of Antiquaries of London, *A Collection of Ordinances and Regulations*, pp. 151-153.

[2] Charlotte Isabelle Merton, *The Women Who Served Queen Mary and Queen Elizabeth*, p. 64.

bath houses at Whitehall and Hampton Court, although we may assume they certainly did since we know that Henry VIII himself enjoyed regular baths. The 1542 Whitehall inventory recorded a list of "sundry linen serving for His Grace in his bath."[3]

At the Tudor court, there were three ranks of toilet. The royals and nobles would use the close-stool, a lidded chamber pot set in a padded box. Several close-stools belonging to Henry VIII were inventoried; some were stuffed with swansdown, covered with black velvet and held together with gilt nails.[4] The King's sixth wife, Katherine Parr, had an opulent lavatory with a seat of crimson velvet.[5]

The "stool room", where the close-stool was placed, had two doors, one leading to the owner's bedchamber and one to the outdoors for servants to remove the waste. Henry VIII's fifth wife, Katharine Howard, used her stool room for clandestine meetings with her ex-fiancé, Thomas Culpeper.

At the head of Henry VIII's Privy Chamber stood the groom of the stool, the body servant who carried the traditional duties of intimate attendance on the King when he made use of the royal close-stool. The only time this term was

---

[3] Maria Hayward, *Dress at the Court of King Henry VIII*, p. 107.
[4] Lacey Baldwin Smith, *A Tudor Tragedy*, p. 92.
[5] Linda Porter, *Katherine the Queen*, p. 153.

used in reference to the Queen's female servants was in 1598 when Katherine Carey Howard was recorded as being Queen Elizabeth's "groom of the stool".[6]

Dressing

All of Henry VIII's wives were dressed in magnificence expressly for display and understood the link between sumptuous dress and the fitness to rule. According to the sumptuary laws, only the royal family was allowed to wear cloth of gold and the colour purple. Dressing a Tudor queen was a private ceremony with a handful of her closest female servants in attendance. This private ritual behind closed doors would evolve during the reign of King George II into a "lever", a formal ceremony of dressing the monarch and his consort in the presence of servants and courtiers. It differed from the pompous French dressing ceremony but in many instances was similar; it was restricted to the members of the bedchamber with a set of strict, hierarchical rules.[7]

One may only wonder if some parts of this elaborate ritual were borrowed from earlier periods. If this was indeed

---

[6] Charlotte Isabelle Merton, *The Women Who Served Queen Mary and Queen Elizabeth*, p. 65.

[7] Hannah Smith, *Georgian Monarchy: Politics and Culture, 1714-1760*, pp. 100-101.

the case, then we may assume that placing certain garments on the Queen's body was hierarchical, which means that the highest ranking lady would pass each garment to the dressers—ladies of equally high rank who would put them on the Queen—and the lowest ranking ladies would hold and later put the shoes on the Queen's feet. However, that's only an educated guess; the sources concerning the dressing ritual within the Queen's chamber are scant.

According to the Eltham Ordinances, the King's clothes were brought from the Wardrobe of the Robes by the Yeoman of the Wardrobe. However, the Yeoman of the Wardrobe was not admitted to the King's presence but handed the clothes through the door to one of the grooms, who, in turn, passed them on to the Gentlemen of the Privy Chamber.

Interestingly, none of the grooms or ushers were allowed to "approach or presume (unless they be otherwise by His Grace commanded or admitted) to lay hands upon his royal person, or intermeddle with preparing or dressing of the same, but only the said six gentlemen [of the Privy Chamber] except it to be to warm the clothes, or to bring to the said gentlemen such things as shall appertain to the apparelling and dressing of the King's said person".[8] Understandably, the same ritual was observed within the Queen's chambers, with

---

[8] Society of Antiquaries of London, *A Collection of Ordinances and Regulations*, p. 156.

only her closest ladies in attendance. The dressing ritual would usually take place within the bedchamber or Privy Chamber in the early Tudor period; special rooms known as "raying" or "dressing" chambers, where a royal personage was attired, became popular during the early 1530s onwards.[9]

Female dress during the Tudor period consisted of several layers of clothing. First, a chemise or shift made of white linen was placed next to the wearer's skin. Over her shift, the wearer would put on a petticoat of scarlet. Then, a sleeveless kirtle with a stiffened bodice was placed to lift the décolletage in a fashionable way. Here's where the nimble fingers of the ladies-in-waiting were lacing the Queen's bodice in front, back or on the side depending on where the gown would fasten.

Under the front lacing of the bodice, one of the ladies would place a stomacher—a richly embroidered triangular panel that filled in the front opening—and another would pin it in place. A hooped farthingale—a structure used to support and shape the skirts into the desired style—would be put in place before the outer gown would be donned. A triangular shaped forepart—an apron-like panel made of the most exquisite materials, such as satin or cloth of gold—would be

---

[9] Howard Montagu Colvin, *The History of the King's Works, Volume 3 Part 1*, p. 266.

fastened or pinned onto the kirtle and be visible from under the gown.

The Queen's legs would be warmed with a pair of woollen stockings or hose held in place by garters made from silken ribbon. Around the waist, a girdle belt with a long beaded chain would be placed. A small pomander filled with perfume or herbs, or a little prayer book would have been attached at the end of the chain.

Once the dressing was complete and the Queen's slippers, made of black velvet, were prised onto her feet, attention would have turned to her head. Small French hoods with long silken veils were very popular at court, revealing a generous amount of hair in front; gable hoods were equally popular, although some contemporaries opined that they were too heavy and unbecoming even for attractive women. All of the Queen's headgears were richly adorned with gems and pearls.

Jewellery worn by royal consorts passed from one queen to the other, and Henry VIII often gave orders to reset it for the use of his subsequent wives. When the King ordered Katherine of Aragon to return her queenly jewels to bestow them on Anne Boleyn before he presented her as his future bride in Calais in 1532, Katherine vehemently protested and said that "it was against her conscience to give her jewels to adorn a person who is the scandal of Christendom", but she was pressed and eventually gave in.[10] Anne Boleyn proudly wore the queenly jewels before her coronation, causing outrage at court. "She keeps the Queen's jewels, and there is nothing said about returning them", the imperial ambassador observed in February 1533, adding later on that "it seems a very strange thing to everyone, and very cruel, that the King should allow the Queen to be so despoiled of her jewels, and give them to another".[11]

Some ladies-in-waiting were appointed as keepers of the Queen's jewels; Anne Herbert—Katherine Parr's sister— had "duly accounted for all and delivered the same at the King's palace of Westminster" after Katherine Howard's downfall.[12]

Mass

Once dressed and adorned as befitted her status, the Queen and her ladies would attend the morning mass. The Queen had her own private oratory within her suite of rooms, known as the Privy Closet or "the Queen's closet", where she

---

[10] *Letters and Papers*, Volume 5, note 1377.
[11] *Letters and Papers*, Volume 6, note 142.
   Ibid., note 391.
[12] *Letters and Papers*, Volume 17, note 283.

could worship in private. In an age when religion saturated everyday life, all of Henry VIII's wives were very pious. The Catholic Katherine of Aragon rose at midnight to be present at matins and made ready at five o'clock in the morning "saying that the time was lost which was spent in apparelling herself". She attended mass daily and "prayed kneeling on her knees without cushions". Underneath her royal attire, she wore "the habit of St. Francis"—a penitential hair shirt.[13] Katherine's successor, Anne Boleyn, was deemed as "the principal cause of the spread of Lutheranism in this country" by the imperial ambassador, Eustace Chapuys, although she was not a Lutheran.[14]

It seems that divine service did not always command undivided attention, and it was accepted by most courtiers that both Henry VIII and Anne Boleyn were not enthusiastic sermon gadders. The Archbishop of Canterbury warned Hugh Latimer that he should "stand no longer in the pulpit than an hour, or an hour and a half at the most" because "by long expense of time, the King and the Queen shall, peradventure,

---

[13] The details related by Jane Dormer, one of the maids of honour serving in the household of Mary Tudor, Katherine of Aragon's daughter. Henry Clifford, *The Life of Jane Dormer, Duchess of Feria*, p. 73.
[14] *Calendar of State Papers, Spain*, Volume 5 Part 2, note 43.

wax so weary at the beginning that they shall have small delight to continue throughout with you to the end".[15]

Breakfast

Upon her return, the Queen would break her fast; it was considered inappropriate to do this before attending mass if she intended to participate fully in the liturgy and take Holy Communion since the Church's regulations stipulated that the night fast should not be broken prior to receiving Communion. This procedure did not change even though Henry VIII had broken off with the Catholic Church in 1533.[16]

Messes—whole menus for a small group of individuals—were prepared by Tudor cooks for the Queen and her female staff. Breakfast, however, was not a formal meal, and it was not listed in the Eltham Ordinances under "messes". A typical Tudor breakfast served within the royal suite of rooms consisted of bread (sometimes soaked in wine), cheese and beef and various fish. The choice between meat, fish and "white meat" (eggs and cheese) was determined by

---

[15] G.W. Bernard, *Anne Boleyn*, p. 115.

[16] When the Venetian ambassadors visited the court in 1515, they reported: "they led us into a sort of hall [the Great Hall], and though it was before mass, they made us breakfast, for fear we should faint". Sebastiano Giustiniani, *Four Years at the Court of Henry VIII*, p. 85.

the liturgical calendar. Eating meat was forbidden on Fridays, and during Lent, meat, cheese and eggs were forbidden as well. Katherine of Aragon "fasted all Fridays and Saturdays and all the Eves of our Blessed Lady with bread and water".[17]

Reading time

After breakfast, the Queen was free to do whatever pleased her best. At first, she may have taken a look at petitions of subjects entreating her to intercede with the King on their behalf and read recent letters. All of Henry VIII's wives—except the teenage Katherine Howard—were highly cultured and enjoyed reading books.

Anne Boleyn delighted in reading anticlerical works and marked passages in William Tyndale's *The Obedience of a Christian Man* to show them to the King. She had also lent this title to one of her maids of honour, Anne Gainsford, but Cardinal Wolsey obtained it from one of his servants, who caught Mistress Gainsford while she was reading it.

William Latymer, Anne's chaplain, wrote that she was "exercising herself continually in reading the French Bible and other French books of like effect and conceived great pleasure in the same, wherefore Her Highness charged her chaplains to

---

[17] Henry Clifford, *The Life of Jane Dormer, Duchess of Feria*, p. 73.

be furnished of all kind of French books that reverently treated of the Holy Scripture."[18] Latymer also said that Anne kept a Bible opened at her desk in the Privy Chamber, encouraging her ladies to read it whenever they wanted to; her copy of William Tyndale's English Bible is currently stored at the British Library.

Katherine Parr owned many books, including a "book of prayers, covered with purple velvet and garnished with gold". She was very religious and held Bible study meetings with her ladies-in-waiting on a daily basis. "Every day is like Sunday", one contemporary observer noted about the religious activities within Katherine Parr's household, "which is a thing hitherto unheard of, especially in a royal palace".[19]

Needlework

In the long hours spent together, the Queen and her ladies devoted their time and energy to all kinds of needlework and embroidery. It was one of the favourite pastimes of Tudor women, and all of Henry VIII's wives were deft with a needle. Katherine of Aragon was responsible for introducing the Spanish taste in embroidery and enjoyed

---

[18] Eric Ives, *The Life and Death of Anne Boleyn*, p. 268.

[19] David Starkey, *Six Wives: The Queens of Henry VIII*, p. 749.

making shirts for Henry VIII. The King was fond of Katherine's shirts and sent her cloth to produce new ones despite the divorce proceedings. When Anne Boleyn learned that her rival was still performing a wifely duty, she threw a public scene and "abused the bearer [of the cloth] in the King's very presence, threatening that she would have him punished severely".[20] Anne stepped in and started sewing shirts for Henry herself, but at some point, the King ordered new ones to be made for him and his male servants by a practised seamstress.[21]

During the reign of Anne's daughter, Elizabeth, the need to redeem the Queen's mother emerged, and one of Anne Boleyn's former chaplains related how Anne was said to have ordered "a great quantity of canvas to be made into shirts and smocks and sheets to those of the poor". Interestingly, she commanded her ladies and maids of honour to sew them "with their own hands".[22]

If sewing shirts was not Anne's forte, she was skilled when it came to embroidery. A rich cushion embroidered with honeysuckle, acorns, Anne's motto and the initials "H" and "A" was recorded in the 1547 inventory of royal goods. George Wyatt, one of the first writers to pen Anne Boleyn's biography,

---

[20] *Calendar of State Papers, Spain*, Volume 4 Part 1, note 354.
[21] David Starkey, *Six Wives: The Queens of Henry VIII*, p. 434.
[22] *Volume 39 of Camden Fourth Series*, p. 54.

recorded that Hampton Court was adorned with "the rich and exquisite works for the greater part wrought by [her] own hand and needle, and also of her ladies".[23]

When Katherine of Aragon was exiled from court and lived out her days in retirement, it was reported that she spent her dreary years "in much prayer, great alms and abstinence; and when she was not this way occupied, then was she, and her gentlewomen, working with their own hands, something wrought in needlework, costly and artificially, which she intended, to the honour of God, to bestow on some of the churches".[24]

Needlework was often presented as a gift by the Queen's women to the King, family and friends, and was to be judged in terms of the cash value, craftsmanship and affectionate care intended. During the Christmas season of 1534, Anne Boleyn's sister-in-law, for instance, gave the King a shirt with a collar of silver work.[25]

---

[23] Eric Ives, *The Life and Death of Anne Boleyn*, p. 253.
[24] Agnes Strickland, *Memoirs of the Queens of Henry VIII, and His Mother, Elizabeth of York*, p. 9.
[25] Eric Ives, *The Life and Death of Anne Boleyn*, p. 216.

Music and dance

When not sewing or embroidering, the Queen would indulge in listening to music, playing instruments and dancing. Music was an integral part of court ceremony and entertainment, religious services and private pleasure. Trumpeters provided fanfares and ceremonial music, and the royal musicians, usually employed in groups, played within the King's and Queen's Private Chambers and upon occasions of state.

Minstrels—professional musicians who played the lute, rebec, harp, viol and trumpet—were employed by the royal couple to put on informal concerts within the privacy of their chambers. They were also employed to teach royal children and young courtiers, although Katherine of Aragon's daughter, Mary, who took pleasure in playing the lute and spinet, was known to personally teach many of her maids of honour to play.[26]

Anne Boleyn sang well, knew how to accompany herself on the lute and owned a pair of clavichords, which she decorated with green ribbon.[27] She was known for her love of music and dancing, with hostile sources noting that "her life was passed most in masks, dancing, plays and such corporal

---

[26] *Calendar of State Papers, Venice*, Volume 5, note 934.
[27] *Letters and Papers*, Volume 10, note 913.

delights, in which she had a special grace".[28] One Spanish source relates how she "ostentatiously tried to attract to her service the best-looking men and best dancers to be found".[29] This statement was based on the fact that one of Anne's musicians, Mark Smeaton, was accused of adultery with her and—after being tortured—confessed to having known her carnally. He never recanted his statement, hoping, perhaps, for a pardon if he cooperated with the authorities.

Upon learning of Mark's confession, Anne said that "he was never in my chamber but at Winchester, and there I sent for him to play the virginals, for there my chamber was above the King's", underlining that even if they were alone, Henry VIII would have known that Mark played for Anne instead of seducing her.[30] During her trial, Anne Boleyn was also accused of having held dancing parties in her bedchamber.[31] Proof of adultery was collected from the fact that Anne was handed from one man to another in the course of the dance.

Anne's brother, George, was accused of incest with her based on the fact that he "took her by the hand and led her into the dance among the other ladies", handing her down to

---

[28] Henry Clifford, *The Life of Jane Dormer, Duchess of Feria*, p. 78.

[29] *Chronicle of King Henry VIII (The Spanish Chronicle)*, p. 55.

[30] Elizabeth Norton, *Anne Boleyn In Her Own Words*, p. 246.

[31] *Calendar of State Papers Foreign*, Elizabethan, Volume 1, note 1303.

subsequent partners.[32] The charges were far-fetched because dancing with one's brother was not perceived as unusual; years later, Katherine Parr danced with her brother "very gracefully", and no one thought it was scandalous.[33] Nevertheless, Anne Boleyn, her brother, the musician and three men of the King's Privy Chamber were sentenced to death in one of the bloodiest coups in English history.

Katherine Howard, Henry VIII's fifth wife and the second of his queens to be executed for adultery, was also famous for her pastimes. When, shortly before her arrest she kept to her chambers, the French ambassador reported that "before . . . she did nothing but dance and rejoice, but now when the musicians come, they are told there is no time to dance".[34]

Gambling

In a lighter vein, the Queen and her ladies entertained themselves by playing chess, cards and dice, and they often gambled for small amounts of money. One anecdote says that when Katherine of Aragon played cards with Anne Boleyn and the latter frequently turned up a king, the Queen remarked:

---

[32] Ibid.

[33] Pedro de Gante, *Narrative of the Visit of the Duke of Najera*, p. 11.

[34] David Starkey, *Six Wives: The Queens of Henry VIII*, p. 434.

"My lady Anne, you have good hap to stop at king, but you are not like others, you will have all or none".[35] The anecdote might be more than apocryphal considering the fact that Anne was an excellent card player, and the King lost a great deal of money to her.[36]

Mealtime

Unlike the rest of the court, who were usually dining in the Great Hall starting at ten in the morning, Tudor queens did not have fixed mealtimes. On a typical day, the Queen would dine in her Privy Chamber, served by high-ranking ladies-in-waiting. The Queen's women did not fetch the food because that was the job of gentleman ushers. Similarly, if the Queen was hungry in between meals, the ushers would fetch her some bread and ale from the buttery, pantry or cellar and hand it to the ladies at the door of the Queen's apartments.[37]

Dinner within the Queen's apartments was a private ritual. The Lisle letters give us a glimpse of Jane Seymour's dinner, revealing that the Countesses of Rutland and Sussex

---

[35] Eric Ives, *The Life and Death of Anne Boleyn*, p. 100.
[36] Ibid., p. 217.
[37] Society of Antiquaries of London, *A Collection of Ordinances and Regulations*, p. 157.

were "waiters on Her Grace" on one occasion.[38] What exactly their role was remains unknown considering the fact that Tudor queens had male carvers, servers and cup-bearers in their households who tended to their needs at the table. Perhaps male servants performed their duties during grand feasts, banquets and other stately occasions when the Queen dined in public, and the ladies-in-waiting performed light duties such as pouring the wine or holding "a fine cloth before the Queen's face when she listed to spit or do otherwise at her pleasure."[39] This view is sustained by evidence from Queen Elizabeth's reign; when the Queen dined privately, she was waited upon by her ladies, although male staff served her on grand occasions of state. Bridget Manners acted as the Queen's carver, and Mary Howard was appointed as her cup-bearer.[40]

Before each meal, the Queen would wash her hands in rosewater because she would mostly use her fingers during the meal. Knives and spoons were provided at table, but forks were not commonly used in England until the eighteenth century.

---

[38] Read more in Chapter 2.

[39] *Letters and Papers*, Volume 6, note 601.

[40] Violet A. Wilson, *Queen Elizabeth's Maids of Honour and Ladies of the Privy Chamber*, p. 192.

Eating meat without a dispensation was forbidden during Lent and every Friday and Saturday. The usual royal fare consisted of mutton, venison, veal, swan, stork, goose and all sorts of fish. Anne Boleyn was known to ask for shrimp and carp from Cardinal Wolsey's fishponds to eat during Lent, and the Lisle family shipped delicacies such as dotterels to satisfy her gourmet palate.[41] Jane Seymour developed a craving for quails during her pregnancy, and they, too, were shipped by the Lisles from Calais. Drinks such as ale, beer and wine would be drunk from silver or gilt goblets and meat served on gold or silver plates.

Sport

Outdoor pursuits were not neglected. Walking in the gardens, riding, hunting, archery and hawking were the most popular sports during the Tudor period. Henry VIII excelled in equestrian arts: he was "a capital horseman and a fine jouster".[42] The Venetian ambassador praised the King's accomplishments and physique:

"He was extremely fond of hunting, and never took that diversion without tiring eight or ten horses, which he

---

[41] Eric Ives, *The Life and Death of Anne Boleyn*, pp.111, 212.
[42] Patrick Williams, *Katharine of Aragon*, p. 171.

caused to be stationed beforehand along the line of country he meant to take."[43]

The term "hunting" did not refer solely to deer hunting, something that is conjured up in the modern mind upon hearing this word, but applied to different styles of the slaughter of wildlife. There was also a significant difference between the hunting styles employed by men and women. When a Tudor woman went hunting, she would set off to a nearby vantage point to aim at already imparked animals, usually deer.[44]

Hunting "par force" was considered the noblest form of hunting; huntsmen on horseback and on foot pursued the selected animal with hounds. It was considered a lucky outcome when the game was killed by hounds and not slain with a sword or a hunting knife by one of the hunters. Hounds formed an important part of the chase, and Henry VIII established a post of Master of the Buckhounds, held notably by George Boleyn from 1528 to 1536.[45]

Henry VIII built a hilltop hunting Great Standing, a three-storey building without walls used to shoot and watch

---

[43] Ibid.

[44] Charlotte Isabelle Merton, *The Women Who Served Queen Mary and Queen Elizabeth*, p. 64.

[45] Albert Stewart Barrow, *Monarchy and the Chase*, p. 57.

the "par force" hunting at Chingford in Epping Forest.[46] It was there in July 1532 when the French ambassador joined Henry VIII and Anne Boleyn on a hunting trip. He reported that the King sometimes placed Anne with him, together with their crossbows, to shoot the deer as they passed, "and in other places to see coursing".[47] Henry VIII enjoyed hunting escapades with Anne during their courtship since they provided a rare opportunity to snatch some private moments in the bosom of nature. The imperial ambassador reported that Anne always accompanied Henry during hunting parties and, what was particularly unusual, "without any female attendants of her own".[48]

One of the most popular indoor sports was tennis. The Venetian ambassador reported that "it was the prettiest thing in the world to see him [Henry VIII] play; his fair skin glowing through a shirt of the finest texture."[49] It was a sport reserved for men only, and women were confined to the role of spectators but were free to bet on their favourite players. While Anne Boleyn was watching and betting on a game of tennis at Greenwich, she was summoned before the council, arrested and taken to the Tower; she was beheaded a few weeks later.

---

[46] Nicholas Hagger, *A View of Epping Forest*, p. 66.
[47] *Letters and Papers*, Volume 5, note 1187.
[48] *Calendar of State Papers, Spain*, Volume 4 Part 2, note 765.
[49] Patrick Williams, *Katharine of Aragon*, p. 171.

It was not an unusual sight to see the Queen and her ladies walking in the gardens with their dogs. Large dogs such as greyhounds and mastiffs were allowed at court, but the Eltham Ordinances banned all dogs except ladies' spaniels from the precincts of the court. If courtiers did obtain the royal permission to bring their dogs with them, they had to keep them in kennels.

Anne Boleyn had a lapdog named Purkoy and was very upset when he fell out of a window and died. The imperial ambassador mocked little Purkoy's death when he reported that upon hearing the latest unfavourable news from France in 1535, Henry VIII, Anne Boleyn and their adherents were astounded "like dogs falling out of a window".[50] Anne also owned a large greyhound which savaged a cow on a hunting trip.

Katherine of Aragon was the proud owner of a pet monkey, a novelty at the time, but Anne Boleyn confessed that she "loved no such beasts" nor could "abide the sight of them".[51] Henry VIII obviously did not share Anne's opinion since he also kept a monkey. Exotic animals such as peacocks and pelicans were brought to the King out of the New Found Land and were kept in coops at Greenwich Palace in 1534.

---

[50] *Letters and Papers*, Volume 9, 357.
[51] *Letters and Papers*, Volume 8, 1084.

Anne Boleyn had often complained that the birds' noise bothered her, and she could not sleep in the mornings.

Bedtime

Over the normal course of events, the King would spend each night with the Queen. Interestingly, they would sleep together within the Queen's chambers, or more accurately, in the King's chamber abutting the Queen's bedchamber. Henry VIII's infatuation with Anne Boleyn and his subsequent quest for divorce from Katherine of Aragon meant that the royal couple ceased to sleep together, although at some point in 1528, the King's advisers counselled him to sleep with Katherine "for fear his opponents should allege that he is acting in defiance of the Queen's conjugal rights". Henry VIII listened to this advice and kept visiting Katherine of Aragon's chambers, staying for the night.[52] The Queen never revealed what happened behind those closed doors. Did she and Henry VIII resume sexual relations despite the fact that the King was in love with Anne Boleyn? If so, Anne must have been furious; she famously denied granting Henry's sexual desires until their wedding night.

---

[52] *Calendar of State Papers, Spain*, Volume 3 Part 2, note 600.

We do not know when exactly the royal couple would go to sleep each night, but one account reveals that when Katherine of Aragon was sent away from court in 1531, the King's councillors came to her "towards eight or nine o'clock at night, just as the Queen was going to bed".[53] However, Katherine was living in exile, spending much time on prayer while the court was lavishly entertained, and we may assume that Anne Boleyn went to sleep much later.

---

[53] *Calendar of State Papers, Spain*, Volume 4 Part 2, note 739.

Part 2: Women who served the six wives of Henry VIII

Chapter 5:

The Spanish Household of Katherine of Aragon, 1501-09

When Katherine of Aragon came to England in November 1501, she was a sixteen-year-old Spanish princess who was about to wed Prince Arthur, Henry VII's heir. She brought with her a large household, more grand and lavish than that of Henry VII's wife, Elizabeth of York. After the wedding, most of her royal entourage was sent back to Spain, but Katherine's ladies, hand-picked by her mother, Isabella of Castile, were to stay with her. Dona Elvira Manuel held the offices of Katherine of Aragon's First Lady of Honour and First Lady of the Bedchamber.[1] She was Katherine's closest female attendant and governess, and was to be consulted about everything concerning Katherine's household. As a lady of high rank herself, Dona Elvira had her own Lady of Company—the equivalent of an English lady-in-waiting—and two female servants to attend upon her everyday needs. Dona Catalina Cardenas, about whom very little is known, was Katherine of Aragon's chief lady-in-waiting who was "to

---

[1] *Calendar of State Papers, Spain*, Volume 1, note 288.

attend on her in her private rooms".[2] Five maids of honour were supervised by Catalina de Montoya, who held a similar position as the English Mother of Maids. Two Moorish slaves were to attend the maids and two "servants in the rooms of the Princess" served as chamberers.[3]

Katherine of Aragon's wedding to Prince Arthur took place on 12 November 1501. She was accompanied by "a good number of lords, knights, gentlemen and ladies" and was conducted to St. Paul's Cathedral by the ten-year-old Duke of York—the future Henry VIII—and the Count of Cabra, who came with her from Spain. Cecily of York, daughter of Edward IV and Elizabeth of York's younger sister, carried Katherine's long train.

Shortly after Katherine of Aragon's wedding, many members of her household were sent back to Spain. Henry VII, always ready to cut costs whenever the situation required, decided that the young Princess did not need such a lavish entourage. Katherine, naturally, was "annoyed and pensive" at their departure, but Henry VII decided to lift her spirits.[4] He summoned her and her ladies to his vast library and showed them books and then "provided a jeweller . . . with many rings with precious stones and huge diamonds and jewels of most

---

[2] Ibid.

[3] Ibid.

[4] Patrick Williams, *Katharine of Aragon*, p. 115.

goodly fashion, every one of them being of great richness and treasure."[5] Then, he asked Katherine to "look over them and behold them carefully, and then to choose one of them that she most liked. And after she had chosen her pleasure, every lady of Spain who was with her made their own choices, and the remaining jewels were given to the English ladies".[6] The King's plan worked, and Katherine's mood changed for the better.

Katherine's marriage to Arthur was short lived. After a mysterious illness, the fifteen-year-old Prince died on 2 April 1502, leaving Katherine a young widow. She was about to face seven years of penurious widowhood, becoming a pawn in diplomatic machinations between her parents, Ferdinand of Aragon and Isabella of Castile, and her father-in-law, Henry VII. Katherine of Aragon was now the Dowager Princess of Wales, but her future was uncertain.

Katherine's parents were eager to see her married to Henry VII's younger son, Prince Henry, now heir to the throne, and in May 1502, despatched their extraordinary ambassador to put the proposal to Henry VII. The plan was in motion even before Katherine of Aragon revealed that her marriage to Arthur was unconsummated, and—although her confessor claimed otherwise—she instructed Dona Elvira Manuel to

---

[5] Ibid.
[6] Ibid.

write to her mother, Isabella, to affirm that she was still a virgin.

In July 1502, Queen Isabella instructed the Spanish ambassador, Ferdinand, Duke of Estrada, to keep the negotiations going. She also included a set of regulations touching upon Katherine's household:

"See, moreover, that the King of England give immediately to the Princess of Wales, our daughter, whatever may be necessary for her maintenance and that of her people. Provide also that, in the arrangement of her household, everything should be done to the satisfaction of the King of England. Take care that Dona Elvira remains with her, and any other persons whom she may wish to retain, according to the number which was agreed upon for her service."[7]

Despite Katherine's claim that she was a virgin, no one investigated whether that was indeed the case. Her servants were not questioned, and no diplomatic assessment had been made as to whether the Dowager Princess of Wales was speaking the truth. Perhaps it did not matter at all; what mattered at the time was that the Anglo-Spanish alliance was maintained by all means and that Katherine was to become the wife of Henry VII's younger son, Prince Henry. The

---

[7] *Calendar of State Papers, Spain*, Volume 1, note 327.

question of Katherine's virginity would eventually return to haunt her thirty years later.

Quarrelling servants

During the summer of 1503, Katherine of Aragon experienced problems within her own household; her servants could not "live in peace with one another".[8] Additionally, her health had begun to deteriorate, and Henry VII took it upon himself to help Katherine; he sent her his servants and wrote her a letter in which he declared that he was "ready to do all in his power for her".[9] Katherine's problems were, perhaps, caused by her warring servants, and several days later, to change her environment, Henry VII took Katherine on a summer progress. They hunted together, and it seemed that Katherine's health improved while she was far away from her household.

Then she fell ill again and suffered from "ague and derangement of the stomach"; three days later, she was able to travel again, this time accompanied by the King, his daughter Mary and the English ladies-in-waiting.[10] Katherine enjoyed good health for several days, but as her separation with the

---

[8] Ibid., note 400.
[9] Ibid., note 397.
[10] Ibid., note 398.

royal family was nearing, she fell ill again, much more seriously than before. Henry VII was unable to stay until Katherine's health improved because he was obliged to attend business in Kent.

Still unwell, Katherine returned to her household, but the King kept sending his letters and even physicians to take care of her. Seeing the King's kindness, Katherine wrote to Henry VII to aid her with the growing tensions in her household, but the King politely refused. They were not his subjects to command; the best solution was to entrust this matter to the Spanish ambassador, who, in turn, would intercede with Katherine's parents on her behalf.[11]

The influence of Dona Elvira Manuel

It seemed that the tensions in the household were caused, mostly, by financial matters. Katherine was too liberal in spending money, and the Spanish ambassador, Rodrigo de Puebla, opined that "nothing should be done or expended against the wishes and opinion of Dona Elvira" who should be presented with accounts of all "what has been spent".[12] De Puebla was Dona Elvira's supporter and did everything he

---

[11] Ibid., note 400.
[12] Ibid., note 401.

could to enforce her discipline over Katherine's household; "as far as lies in my power, I will increase her authority", he declared to Katherine's parents.

That increasing Dona Elvira's authority was necessary is attested in his despatch from October 1504. King Henry VII had sent a golden headdress to Dona Elvira; it was a splendid garment sent as a token of favour. The King only sent such a gift to his closest female relatives, namely his mother or daughters. "This headdress was not given her in secret", de Puebla continued, "but in the presence of the Princess and of her ladies, in order to invest her with as much authority as I could".[13]

In the autumn of 1504, Katherine of Aragon stayed at court for twenty days. De Puebla reported that she "is keeping the same rule and observance and seclusion which she did before in her own house, in accordance with the wishes and desires of Dona Elvira Manuel".[14] The English were not used to such a strict manner of bringing a royal child up, but it seemed they approved of it. "This manner of proceeding is thought well of by all the kingdom, and much more by the King", wrote

---

[13] Ibid.
[14] Ibid., note 420.

de Puebla, adding that Henry VII commanded Katherine should be treated as if she were his own daughter.[15]

Henry VII was as good as his word and ordered his eight-year-old daughter Mary to be "attended in the same way as the Princess of Wales".[16] Unfortunately, we do not know what this treatment was. De Puebla reported that during Katherine's visit to court, "some persons"—who, he did not explain—desired to convince her that "she need not observe such order and seclusion" as imposed on her by Dona Elvira, and "that she ought to enjoy greater freedom".[17] Dona Elvira was, apparently, worried about those "persons" whose whispers into Katherine's ear threatened to undermine her position, and she wrote a letter to Ferdinand and Isabella, detailing the situation within Katherine's household. Unfortunately, the letter does not survive.

Katherine was, however, entirely subjected to Dona Elvira's will and allowed her to make important decisions. When one of Katherine's Spanish maids, Maria de Rojas, was courted by an Englishman, Katherine was overjoyed. She wanted Maria, who was her close companion and a bedfellow, to remain in England. The prospective groom was none other

---

[15] Ibid.
[16] Ibid., note 406.
[17] Ibid., note 420.

than Thomas Stanley, second Earl of Derby, a grandson and only heir of Henry VII's stepfather.

According to the Spanish ambassador, Derby was "the best match in the kingdom".[18] Henry VII gave his blessing to this match, although he did not want to meddle as Maria was not an English subject. Maria de Rojas was an heiress to a wealthy Spanish landowner and a valuable catch. Dona Elvira was well aware of this fact, and she decided to arrange a match between Maria and her own son, Don Antonio. "It is a strange and unbecoming affair", wrote the disgusted Spanish ambassador.[19]

Maria de Rojas eventually left England and returned to Spain. In 1531, she was married to Alvaro de Mendoza and was thought to live in Najera, Vitoria or Madrid; she had been sought to give a testimonial concerning the consummation of the marriage between Katherine of Aragon and Prince Arthur.[20]

In the summer of 1505, Dona Elvira Manuel betrayed Katherine's trust. She and her brother, Juan Manuel, engineered a plan to damage the interests of Katherine's father, Ferdinand of Aragon, by facilitating the meeting

---

[18] Ibid.
[19] Ibid., note 439.
[20] Giles Tremlett, *Catherine of Aragon*, p. 337.

between Philip of Burgundy, Ferdinand's political enemy, and Henry VII. Philip was married to Katherine's sister, Juana the Mad, and Katherine, elated by the prospect of seeing her sister again, naively wrote to Philip to encourage him to arrange the meeting. Katherine was "so much under the influence of Dona Elvira" that she did not even presume that she was being played for a fool.[21]

When Dona Elvira's intrigue was revealed by the Spanish ambassador, Katherine was devastated; she now had to choose between loyalty to her father, who still had not delivered the remaining part of her dowry, and her Lady of the Bedchamber, who was a constant companion and something of a mother-figure. She chose her father and sent Dona Elvira away to the Netherlands, under the pretext of an eye operation.

Struggling to survive

Dona Elvira Manuel's departure was devastating for Katherine and six of her remaining ladies. In December of 1505, Katherine finally wrote a daring letter to her father, detailing her financial situation:

---

[21] *Calendar of State Papers, Spain,* Volume 1, note 440.

"Your Highness already knows how many times I have written to him that since I came to England I have not received a single maravedi [Spanish currency] other than for food, and it was because of this that I have run up many debts in London. What is even more painful to me is to see my servants and ladies-in-waiting suffering and not being able to dress themselves decently."[22]

Katherine was especially concerned with the well-being of her Spanish maids of honour who came to England with her and stayed by her side even when she was penniless. It was a custom to provide marriage portions for unmarried servants, and Katherine took this responsibility very seriously. In September 1505, she pleaded for Maria de Salazar, who had a marriage prospect in front of her but could not be married until her marriage portion was delivered.[23] When Ferdinand of Aragon did not reply, Katherine seemed to lose her patience. She reminded him that the six ladies who "have served me right well and with much necessity" received no payment for their services. Katherine tried to appeal to Ferdinand's sake of decency, reminding him that some of her ladies served her mother, Queen Isabella, "and they served her a long time". Now, they were of marriageable ages, but Katherine had "nothing to give them". Therefore, she

---

[22] Patrick Williams, *Katharine of Aragon*, p. 146.
[23] Mary Anne Everett Wood, *Letters of Royal and Illustrious Ladies of Great Britain*, Volume 1, p. 127.

explained, she expected her father to send money for their marriage portions.[24]

Most of Katherine's ladies endured penury with her even if it meant that they would remain spinsters in an age where marriage and motherhood were deemed to be the highest state to which a woman could aspire. One of them, however, was not prepared to waste her youth and good looks and decided to take matters into her own hands.

Francesca de Caceres was in charge of dressing and undressing Katherine of Aragon, and the latter often confided in her, but when Francesca secretly married a Genoese banker, Katherine never forgave her. Several years later, when Francesca asked Katherine for a recommendation because she wanted to serve at the court of the Archduchess of Austria, Katherine of Aragon's former sister-in-law, Katherine bluntly refused. "It is true that she was my woman before she was married", Katherine recalled, "but now since she cast herself away, I have no more charge of her." Furthermore, Katherine believed that the post in the archduchess's household was not suitable for Francesca because "she is so perilous a woman that it shall be dangerous to put her in a strange house."[25]

---

[24] Ibid., p. 129.
[25] *Letters and Papers*, Volume 1, note 2120.

Henry VII realized that mistreating Katherine of Aragon would put pressure on her father to pay the second installment of her dowry. Caught up in the diplomatic machinations, Katherine's health deteriorated. She believed her life was over; she was not married, she was a stranger in a foreign land with not enough money to buy new clothes—"I was all but naked", she despaired—and contempt was shown to her "when the money of her portion did not arrive". Much to her despair, her servants were short of begging alms.[26] In 1509, however, Katherine's fortunes changed for the better. Henry VII died after a prolonged illness, and his son, the seventeen-year-old Prince Henry, ascended the throne as Henry VIII. One of his first decisions was to marry Katherine of Aragon.

---

[26] Mary Anne Everett Wood, *Letters of Royal and Illustrious Ladies of Great Britain*, Volume 1, p. 139.

Chapter 6:
Katherine the Queen, 1509-31

Most of Katherine of Aragon's ladies were English, but she did not forget about the handful of her Spanish attendants who endured penury with her. Inez de Venegas, Maria de Salinas and Maria de Gravara were among the ladies who played prominent roles in the Queen's household and were notable for their willingness to adapt to the English way of life. The Spanish ambassador was shocked to learn that the few Spaniards who were in Katherine's household "prefer to be friends of the English and neglect their duties to the King of Spain".[1] Among the English ladies who attended Katherine's coronation were Elizabeth Stafford, the sister of the Duke of Buckingham, Margaret Pole, Edward IV's niece, and Elizabeth Boleyn, whose daughter Anne would supplant Katherine as Queen many years later.

As Queen, Katherine of Aragon could finally provide marriage portions for her ladies. Maria de Salinas, Katherine's favourite whom she loved "more than any other mortal", married William Willoughby in 1516.[2] The royal couple

---

[1] *Calendar of State Papers, Spain*, Volume 2, note 201.
[2] Ibid.

financed the marriage, and Katherine of Aragon gave Maria a dowry of 1,100 marks.[3] In 1519, Maria gave birth to her only child, a daughter she named Katherine to honour the Queen.

Royal mistresses

Throughout their marriage, Katherine of Aragon learned to tolerate the King's infidelities and did so with patience and dignity. Although Henry VIII would later fondly recall Katherine's willingness to turn a blind eye on his affairs, at first the Queen struggled to maintain her composure. Henry VIII never flaunted his mistresses openly at court—probably out of respect for his wife—but the first time he took a mistress was a shock to Katherine.

One of her principal ladies-in-waiting, Elizabeth Stafford Radcliffe, Lady Fitzwalter, informed the Queen that her sister, Anne Hastings, had caught the King's wandering eye and that William Compton, Henry's Groom of the Stool, was responsible for arranging meetings between the lovers. Lady Fitzwalter wanted to avoid the scandal and "joined herself with the Duke [of Buckingham], her brother, with her husband and her sister's husband, in order to consult on what should be done in this case." As a consequence, the Duke of

---

[3] Barbara Harris, *English Aristocratic Women*, p. 50.

Buckingham confronted and blamed William Compton for ruining his sister's reputation, but Henry VIII intervened, and the Duke left the court in a huff. Anne Hastings was placed in a convent, but the King was furious.

The Spanish ambassador reported that Henry's rage was directed at Lady Fitzwalter, his mistress's sister, who was promptly dismissed from court. The King also believed that Lady Fitzwalter employed other ladies-in-waiting "to go about the palace insidiously spying out every unwatched moment, in order to tell the Queen [tales]", and he wanted to dismiss all of them but perceived it would cause a scandal at court. With her favourite lady-in-waiting banished, Katherine was furious and "almost all the court knew that the Queen had been vexed with the King, and the King with her, and thus this storm went on between them."[4]

As the years passed by, Katherine of Aragon ignored her husband's mistresses, but when one of them gave birth to the King's illegitimate son, she put up a fight again. The succession of almost annual pregnancies, of which all but one ended either in miscarriage, stillbirth or early death of the infant, had spoiled the Queen's figure and sapped her spirits. The King found consolation in the arms of young Bessie Blount, Katherine's maid of honour. In 1519, Bessie gave birth

---

[4] *Calendar of State Papers, Spain*: Supplement to Volumes 1 and 2, note 8.

to a baby boy, the first and only illegitimate son Henry VIII recognised as his, giving him his name and the surname "Fitzroy", meaning "the King's son". The child was raised as befitted his station and was invested with the title of the Duke of Richmond and Somerset at the age of six. Katherine of Aragon feared that Henry VIII's bastard son would one day be placed above her daughter, Mary, in the Act of Succession, and she openly resented Fitzroy's new titles. The Venetian envoy, Lorenzo Orio, reported that:

"It seems that the Queen resents the earldom and dukedom conferred on the King's natural son and remains dissatisfied, at the instigation, it is said, of three of her Spanish ladies, her chief counsellors, so the King has dismissed them from the court."[5]

Katherine and her Spanish women never understood why the King was so reluctant to accept his daughter, Mary, as the heiress to the throne. They were familiar with the female succession since the Queen's mother and sister had inherited the crown of Castile respectively. In Henry VIII's frame of mind, however, leaving a son instead of a daughter on the throne was essential. The Tudor dynasty was new, with Henry being only the second Tudor monarch to wear a crown. The idea of a female monarch met with hostility in England; in the

---

[5] *Calendar of State Papers, Venice*, Volume 3, note 1053.

twelfth century, Matilda's claim to the throne had led to a long civil war. Unlike Spain, England had never had a successful female ruler, and the King was not ready to accept a girl as his heiress.

Enter Anne Boleyn

In 1527, Katherine of Aragon was faced with Henry VIII's fears that their marriage was sinful. The King was assured by his advisors that his marriage to Katherine was sonless because Katherine was his brother's widow. In fact, however, Henry VIII's decision to annul his marriage was motivated by his infatuation with one of Katherine's maids of honour, Anne Boleyn. Katherine of Aragon knew the Boleyn women well.   Anne's mother, Elizabeth Howard Boleyn, attended the Queen's coronation in 1509 and received a New Year's gift from the King in 1513, which suggests that she was a full-time member of Katherine of Aragon's household.[6] Two of Anne Boleyn's aunts, Elizabeth Wood Boleyn and Anne Tempest Boleyn, served at court as well; the latter attended Katherine of Aragon at the Field of the Cloth of Gold.

If Henry VIII naively believed that Katherine of Aragon would step aside and allow her maid of honour to replace her

---

[6] *Letters and Papers*, Volume 1, notes 82 and 1549.

as the King's wife, he was wrong. Katherine, whose mother was queen in her own right, could not believe that Henry VIII was prepared to risk their daughter's inheritance to beget male heirs by Anne Boleyn. The King, however, wanted to terminate his marriage to Katherine, but he was careful not to reveal that Anne was the cause of his quest for divorce. He kept his feelings for Mistress Boleyn a highly guarded secret, and Anne probably still served as the Queen's maid at the time.

However, only two months after Henry VIII informed Katherine of his plans to divorce her, the whole court knew that Anne Boleyn was his new love. Anne's career as maid of honour came to an end sometime before May 1528 when she was installed in her own chamber at court, far away from Katherine of Aragon's ladies, who suffered from an outbreak of smallpox at the time.[7] In December of that year, the French ambassador reported that "greater court is paid to her every day than has been for a long time paid to the Queen".[8]

Despite the fact that Henry VIII flaunted Anne Boleyn openly at court, he still conducted his royal duties with Katherine of Aragon in public. The Queen presided over the court with him and kept her royal household, while during grand celebrations, Christmas of 1528, for instance, Anne

---

[7] *Letters and Papers*, Volume 4, note 4251.
[8] Ibid., note 5016.

Boleyn avoided meeting Katherine of Aragon.[9] Augustino Scarpinello, a Venetian resident of London who visited the court in the summer of 1530, explained:

"The Queen also is with His Majesty, and they pay each other reciprocally the greatest possible attention, or compliments, in the Spanish fashion with the utmost mental tranquillity, as if there had never been any dispute whatever between them ..."[10]

This was, however, only a façade. Behind closed doors, Katherine fought to preserve her dignity, but whenever she tried to convince Henry to abandon his plans for leaving her, he lashed out at her. She was "mistress in her own household" and had no reason to complain, the King once told her.[11] At first, Katherine deluded herself, believing that her royal husband indeed entertained doubts about the legitimacy of their marriage and hoped that he would eventually abandon the divorce proceedings. "This most virtuous Queen maintains strenuously, that all her King and Lord does, is done by him for true and pure conscience's sake, and not from any wanton appetite", Scarpinello wrote.[12] Several months later, however, she realized that Henry was ruled by passion and complained

---

[9] Ibid.
[10] *Calendar of State Papers, Venice*, Volume 4, note 584.
[11] *Calendar of State Papers, Spain*, Volume 4 Part 1, note 224.
[12] *Calendar of State Papers, Venice*, Volume 4, note 584.

bitterly to him, accusing the King of humiliating her by flaunting his mistress in front of the whole court.[13]

Anne Boleyn was angry with the Queen, and on one occasion, she told Katherine's lady-in-waiting that she wished to see all Spaniards at the bottom of the sea. When the said lady reminded Anne that the Queen was born in Spain, Anne blurted out that she would rather see Katherine of Aragon hanged than acknowledge her either as Queen or the wife of Henry VIII.[14] The seed of rivalry had been sewn, and Anne Boleyn would use her influence to weaken Katherine's resolve. She would, for instance, introduce her trusted ladies into Katherine's household to spy on the Queen.

---

[13] Paul Friedmann, *Anne Boleyn, Vol.1.*, p. 130.
[14] Ibid., p. 129.

Chapter 7:

Household in Exile, 1531-36

During the summer of 1531, Henry VIII decided to send Katherine of Aragon away from court to the More, a residence which formerly belonged to Cardinal Wolsey. Katherine's household was, however, still royal. Mario Savorgnano, an Italian naval commander who was visiting England at the time, paid Katherine a visit and reported that:

"In the morning, we saw her Majesty dine: she had some thirty maids of honour standing round the table, and about fifty who performed its service. Her court consists of about two hundred persons, but she is not so much visited as heretofore, on account of the King."[1]

Two months later, Henry VIII sent a delegation of ministers to urge Katherine to submit to his will and agree to have the divorce case decided in England rather than in Rome. Katherine refused; she knew that the verdict reached in England would be unfavourable to her. She told the ministers that she always believed that her royal husband was pursuing the divorce out of scruples of conscience, but she now realized

---

[1] *Calendar of State Papers, Venice*, Volume 4, note 682.

that Henry was ruled by passion, and therefore she would never agree to impair her daughter's right to the throne. In their despair, the four men went on their knees before the Queen and begged her to agree to Henry VIII's terms. Seeing this, Katherine of Aragon also threw herself on her knees and begged the councillors to remove Anne Boleyn from court and persuade the King to return to her. Ladies and gentlemen of the Queen's household looked on in astonishment, and many shed tears watching Katherine's performance.[2]

Henry VIII had enough of his wife's resistance, and he married Anne Boleyn in secret on 25 January 1533. In April of that year, he sent yet another delegation to urge the Queen to give up her appeal to Rome. When she refused, the councillors informed her that her resistance did not matter anymore because Henry VIII had already married Anne Boleyn. Katherine was shocked: How could her husband marry another woman if he was still married to her? A further blow came when the Queen's chamberlain, William Blount, Baron Mountjoy—who had been married to one of Katherine's Spanish ladies, the now deceased Inez de Venegas—brought more bad news touching upon Katherine's status and her household. The imperial ambassador reported that Mountjoy informed Katherine that:

---

[2] *Letters and Papers,* Volume 5, note 478.

"In future, she should not be called Queen, and that from one month after Easter, the King would no longer provide for her personal expenses or the wages of her servants. He intended her to retire to some private house of her own, and there to live on the small allowance assigned to her, and which, I am told, would scarcely be sufficient to cover the expenses of her household for the first quarter of next year."[3]

Katherine was not intimidated. She replied that "as long as she lived, she would entitle herself Queen" and if the King thought that her expenses were too high, he might "take her own personal property and place her wherever he chose, with a confessor, a physician, an apothecary and two maids for the service of her chamber." And even if that seemed too much to ask, Katherine added, "and there was nothing left for her and her servants to live upon, she would willingly go about the world begging alms for the love of God."[4]

Reorganisation of Katherine's household

In May 1533, the Archbishop of Canterbury proclaimed that Henry VIII's marriage to Katherine of Aragon had been

---

[3] *Calendar of State Papers, Spain*, Volume 4 Part 2, note 1061.
[4] Ibid.

invalid from the beginning. Although Katherine never accepted this judgement, for Henry it was all over: as far as he was concerned, she was always his sister-in-law and never his wife. Anne Boleyn, who was now visibly pregnant, was crowned in June 1533, and the King lavished all his attention on her. In July, Henry VIII issued a proclamation confirming that his marriage to Katherine of Aragon was illegal. Accordingly, Katherine had been deprived of her queenly title:

"The said Lady Katherine may not for the future have or use the name, style, or title, or dignity of Queen of this realm, nor be in any guise reputed, taken or inscribed, by the name Queen of this realm, but by the name, style, title and dignity of Princess Dowager, which name is fitting she should have because she was legitimately married and conjoined with the said Prince Arthur".[5]

Knowing that Katherine had a devoted group of friends and servants, harsh penalties were to be imposed on everyone who would address her as "Queen". Now, Henry VIII proceeded to reorganise Katherine's household. On 30 July 1533, Thomas Cromwell informed Eustace Chapuys that since Katherine "was inexorable, and persisted in her obstinacy without accepting the terms offered to her, however gracious and reasonable, the King considered it his duty to reduce her

---

[5] Patrick Williams, *Katharine of Aragon*, p. 345.

establishment, so that she should no longer have in future a royal suite".[6] The King claimed that Katherine's household had cost him a staggering sum of 40,000 ducats a year. Historian Patrick Williams, author of the recent biography of Katherine of Aragon, dispelled this myth. "In reality", he pointed out, "Katherine had so few servants that the cost was only one-tenth of that figure".[7]

In August 1533, the final reorganisation of Katherine of Aragon's household took place with Henry VIII providing her with a reduced allowance of 30,000 crowns per year, out of which 12,000 would be used to pay the ladies of her chamber. The rest would be administered by a crown-appointed deputy. All of her new servants had taken the oath to her as Princess Dowager, and Katherine, as one can only imagine, was very discontented at this arrangement.[8]

For the latter part of 1533, Katherine was housed at Buckden, with ten ladies-in-waiting to attend upon her. Her most loyal servants refused to call her anything but Queen, and when Henry VIII ordered Baron Mountjoy, Katherine's chamberlain, to identify those obstinate members of her household, he retorted that "it shall not lie in me to accomplish the King's pleasure herein"... "It is not therefore possible for

---

[6] *Calendar of State Papers, Spain*, Volume 4 Part 2, note 1107.

[7] Patrick Williams, *Katharine of Aragon*, p. 349.

[8] *Calendar of State Papers, Spain*, Volume 4 Part 2, note 1117.

me to be a reformer of other folks' tongues, or to accuse them, as I verily believe they are loyal to the King's grace," he said, begging to be relieved of his office.[9]

The King was now furious. Charles Brandon, Duke of Suffolk, was tasked to visit Katherine, extract oaths from her servants, reduce her household and escort her to Somersham, "the most insalubrious and pestilential residence in all England". Suffolk did not agree with his mission. He was now married to Katherine Willoughby, a fourteen-year-old daughter of Maria de Salinas. Maria, who was forced to leave Katherine's service before 1533, kept in contact with Eustace Chapuys, the imperial ambassador, and informed him that Suffolk wished some accident might happen to him on the road that should exempt him from accomplishing the mission.[10]

Katherine confronted the royal emissary "in her great chamber before all the servants of the house". She said she would rather be "hewn in pieces" than deny that she was Henry VIII's wife and the rightful Queen of England.[11] As for moving to Somersham, she said that she would only go to that unhealthy residence if she was carried there by force. And when it came to her household, she would not accept into her

---

[9] *Letters and Papers*, Volume 6, note 1252.
[10] *Calendar of State Papers, Spain*, Volume 4 Part 2, note 1164.
[11] *Letters and Papers*, Volume 6, note 1541.

service anyone who addressed her as "Princess Dowager". Six male servants refused to swear the oath: they were led by Bishop Athequa, Katherine's confessor, and Dr Miguel de la Sa, her physician, both of whom had been with Katherine when she came from Spain in 1501. Eight ladies refused to take the oath: Elizabeth Darrell, Elizabeth Fynes, Elizabeth Otwell, Elizabeth Lawrence, Emma Browne, Margery Otwell, Dorothy Wheler and Blanche Twyforde.[12]

Up until now, the ladies who accompanied Katherine of Aragon to exile were faceless; they were only silhouettes appearing in contemporary reports. However, due to their resistance, their identities were preserved, and today we are able to peek into Katherine of Aragon's chambers and see her surrounded by faithful women who refused to call her anything other but their Queen.

Elizabeth Darrell, Katherine's favourite, was the youngest daughter of Edward Darrell, and she served Katherine before the 1531 exile. By 1533, the members of her immediate family were dead, and Elizabeth had nowhere to stay except in Katherine of Aragon's household. She became known in history as Thomas Wyatt's mistress and muse, the famous "Phyllis".

---

[12] *Letters and Papers*, Volume 7, note 135.

Thomas Wyatt was estranged from his wife, who committed adultery, and was romantically linked with Anne Boleyn before her marriage to Henry VIII. We do not know if Elizabeth Darrell was already involved with Wyatt when she served Katherine of Aragon, but considering the later evidence, she may well have been. Her name appears in Thomas Cromwell's list of "remembrances" from the time of Anne Boleyn's execution in May 1536, where a large payment to Thomas Wyatt is also recorded. Nicola Shulman, author of the recent biography of Thomas Wyatt, believes that both may be connected with reward for Thomas Wyatt's testimony in the Tower during Anne Boleyn's downfall.[13]

After Katherine of Aragon's death, Elizabeth went on to serve Gertrude Courtenay, Marchioness of Exeter. Almost nothing is known about the other ladies who refused to take the oath and betray Katherine of Aragon. The reason for this is that they probably lived unremarkable lives and faded into obscurity, overshadowed by their more famous counterparts.

---

[13] Wyatt was arrested because he was suspected as one of Anne Boleyn's lovers, but he was later released. *The Spanish Chronicle*, a contemporary source written by an anonymous Spanish writer, attributes Wyatt's release to a letter he had written to Henry VIII, in which he reminded the King that he had warned him from marrying Anne Boleyn, who was a "bad woman" and whom Wyatt had known carnally. *Chronicle of King Henry VIII (The Spanish Chronicle)*, pp. 68-70. Nicola Shulman, *Graven with Diamonds*, p. 34.

The ladies who refused to comply with Henry VIII's wishes were dismissed. The imperial ambassador reported:

"They [commissioners] had likewise dismissed every female servant, not leaving even one of her chamber-maids; but hearing the Queen say and affirm that she would take no others into her service, that she would not undress to go to bed, and would lock the door of her chamber herself, they allowed two of them to remain; not those, however, whom the Queen would gladly have chosen."[14]

Katherine of Aragon's household now consisted of an apothecary, a physician, two maids, a confessor and officials appointed by the King. The only thing Suffolk had to do now was pack Katherine's belongings and load them onto carts. Katherine responded by barricading herself in her chambers and challenged the commissioners to break the door down to take her away to Somersham. They did not dare to do this and left. "We find here the most obstinate woman that may be", Suffolk later wrote.[15]

On 17 January 1534, almost a month after Suffolk's visit, Eustace Chapuys reported:

---

[14] *Calendar of State Papers, Spain*, Volume 4 Part 2, note 1165.
[15] *Letters and Papers*, Volume 6, note 1542.

"Ever since the Duke of Suffolk called on her, the Queen has not left her bedroom except for the purpose of hearing mass in a gallery close to her apartments. She has refused to eat or drink anything that her new servants bring her. The little food she takes in this time of tribulation is prepared by her maids-in-waiting within her own bedroom; so that, in point of fact, her sitting-room, bedchamber and kitchen are all in one".[16]

Rumours were rife at court that Henry VIII and Anne Boleyn planned to get rid of Katherine by poisoning her or by planting evidence allowing them to accuse her of high treason. Katherine's health began to deteriorate and, although she had no means of knowing it at the time, she would live only two more years.

"Old, trusty women"

In the spring of 1534, Katherine of Aragon moved to Kimbolton Castle. Her daily routine was punctuated by visits of Henry VIII's councillors trying to convince her to accept Henry's marriage to Anne Boleyn and the Act of Succession after the birth of his new daughter, Elizabeth. Katherine never

---

[16] *Calendar of State Papers, Spain*, Volume 5 Part 1, note 4.

agreed. Her health went downhill at the end of 1535 when she suffered stomach pains and was unable to retain any food.

Katherine of Aragon's Spanish friend, Maria de Salinas, Lady Willoughby, was eager to see her. "I heard that my mistress is very sore sick again", she wrote to Thomas Cromwell in December 1535. She tactfully avoided referring to Katherine as "Queen" but she did not refer to her as "Princess Dowager" either. Instead, she called Katherine her "mistress". "I pray you remember me, for you promised to labour with the King to get me licence to go to her before God send for her, as there is no other likelihood", Maria pleaded.[17]

Cromwell failed to provide the necessary licence, and Maria travelled to Kimbolton Castle on 1 January 1536 without permission. She was distressed and claimed that she had "a fall from her horse within a mile". She tried to gain the sympathies of Katherine's chamberlain and gentleman warden; she thought never to have seen Katherine again "by reason of such tidings as she had heard of her". However, Edmund Bedingfield, a man who controlled access to Katherine, wanted to see the licence. "It was ready to be showed the next morning", Maria assured him and was allowed to enter Katherine of Aragon's chamber.[18]

---

[17] *Letters and Papers*, Volume 9, note 1040.
[18] *Letters and Papers*, Volume 10, note 28.

Although several authors have asserted that Katherine of Aragon died in the arms of Maria de Salinas, there is no evidence to that effect. Bedingfield, who remained in Katherine's service until she died on 7 January 1536, wrote that since Maria de Salinas's brief visit on 1 January, "we never saw her, neither any letters of her licence hither to repair".[19]

The imperial ambassador Chapuys was also eager to see Katherine of Aragon before her death. Unlike Maria de Salinas, he obtained a licence to see her. He arrived on 2 January 1536 and stayed at Kimbolton for four days. Katherine was happy to see him; she would at least "die in his arms and not all alone like a beast".[20] During their first brief meeting, Katherine's chamberlain and steward were also present. Their last meeting was almost private; Chapuys and Katherine talked in Spanish and no one was present except Katherine's "old, trusty women", who, according to Edmund Bedingfield, did not understand Spanish.[21]

English law forbade a wife from making a will during her husband's life, and so Katherine of Aragon ordered her physician to write a short list of requests to be submitted to Henry VIII in lieu of a will. She signed them and handed them to Eustace Chapuys. Even in her dying hour, Katherine did not

---

[19] Ibid.

[20] *Calendar of State Papers, Spain*, Volume 5 Part 2, note 3.

[21] *Letters and Papers*, Volume 10, note 28.

forget about the handful of women who faithfully served her until the end.

She rewarded Elizabeth Darrell with the large sum of £200 "for her marriage", although Elizabeth never married; she remained Thomas Wyatt's mistress until his death in 1542 and bore him at least one illegitimate son.[22] Katherine also bequeathed £100 to "Mistress Blanche"—probably Blanche Twyforde—while Mistresses "Margery" and "Whiller" were given £40 each. We may assume that Mistresses Margery and Whiller were Margery Otwell and Dorothy Whiller, who refused to swear the oath back in December 1533.

Other women who appeared on Katherine of Aragon's list included "Mistress Isabel, daughter of Mistress Margery", "Mistress Mary, my physician's wife", "Sabell of Vergas" and a laundress. There was also a curious bequest to "the little maidens", perhaps dwarfs or jesters.[23] Of all these women, only "Sabell of Vergas" can be satisfyingly identified and her career tracked down in the existing documentation of Katherine of Aragon's household. She was Isabel (or anglicised Elizabeth) Vargas, who was one of Katherine of Aragon's Spanish ladies.[24] She was listed as the Queen's chamberer in

---

[22] Nicholas Harris Nicolas, *Testamenta Vetusta*, Vol. 1, p. 37.
[23] Ibid.
[24] Her surname was variously spelled Vergas, Vargas or Vergus.

October 1511, and six years later, obtained a letter of denization.[25]

We do not know if these ladies-in-waiting were still in Katherine's household at the time of her death. In a letter written to Henry VIII on her deathbed, Katherine urged him to remember her servants:

"I entreat you also, on behalf of my maids, to give them marriage portions, which is not much since there are only three of them. For all my other servants, I ask for one year's pay more than their due, lest they should be unprovided for".[26]

Historian Giles Tremlett believes that the letter is a product of later Catholic propaganda and is, therefore, "almost certainly fictitious".[27] However, the letter written by Katherine shortly before her death is mentioned in a contemporary source describing Katherine's funeral procession. The anonymous author was disgusted that rumours alleging "that in the hour of death, she [Katherine] acknowledged she had not been Queen of England" were spread in England shortly after Katherine's demise. He knew that it was not true "because at that hour, she ordered a writing to be made in her name addressed to the King as her husband, and to the

---

[25] *Letters and Papers*, Volume 1, note 908.
    Letters and Papers, Volume 2, note 2748.
[26] Patrick Williams, *Katharine of Aragon*, p. 374.
[27] Giles Tremlett, *Catherine of Aragon*, p. 422.

ambassador of the Emperor, her nephew, which she signed with these words: Katharine, Queen of England, commending her ladies and servants to the favour of the said ambassador."[28] This account tallies with what we know about Katherine of Aragon's letter—she had indeed addressed it to "my lord and dear husband"—and signed a request to Henry entreating him to be good to her servants. Therefore, we may be certain that Katherine of Aragon died surrounded by the familiar faces of three women who never ceased to call her their Queen.

Katherine's request to be buried at a monastery belonging to her favourite Franciscan Observant Friars had been turned down because the friars' convent no longer existed after Henry VIII's dissolution of monasteries. She was laid to rest in Peterborough Cathedral (now abbey) and honoured as a Dowager Princess of Wales rather than as Queen of England. A succession of solemn masses were celebrated and attended by a variety of noblewomen. The principal among them were Katherine Willoughby Brandon, Duchess of Suffolk (daughter of Maria de Salinas) and Elizabeth Browne Somerset, Countess of Worcester, one of Anne Boleyn's favourite ladies. There were seven chief mourners; Frances de Vere Howard, Countess of Surrey and Eleanor Brandon Clifford, Countess of Cumberland (Henry

---

[28] *Letters and Papers*, Volume 10, note 284.

VIII's niece) among them and nine wives of knights, chambermaids of unspecified number and thirty-six maids of honour.[29]

---

[29] Ibid.

Chapter 8:

Anne Boleyn, Queen-in-waiting, 1527-32

Anne Boleyn could never have envisaged in May 1527 that it would be nearly seven long years before Henry VIII was able to marry her. The King's strongest argument in his quest for divorce was that his conscience was troubled by his marriage to Katherine of Aragon, who was his brother's widow. He believed that his lack of surviving male heirs was due to the fact that the Bible, in the book of Leviticus, stated that a man who married his brother's widow would remain childless. Henry, of course, had a daughter, Princess Mary, but the lack of sons, in his own perception, meant that he was literally childless.

The irony of Henry VIII's situation was that he was eager to apply for a papal dispensation to marry Anne based on a proven degree of affinity with Anne Boleyn's elder sister, Mary, who had previously been his mistress, but he demanded a divorce based on a rumoured degree of affinity between Katherine of Aragon and Prince Arthur. The irony was not lost on courtiers who sympathised with Katherine of Aragon. The fact that Henry stood in the same degree of affinity to Anne as he did to Katherine undermined his credibility, casting Anne Boleyn in the role of a manipulative mistress who desired to topple the Queen from her throne.

Anne was exposed to the hostility of women at court. The French ambassador opined that "if the matter were decided by women, the King would lose the battle".[1] Most women were afraid that if the King could get rid of his wife of twenty years standing, their husbands could do exactly the same. Anne thus became the other woman who ensnared the King, although, as it is clear from Henry VIII's passionate love letters, Anne put up resistance when she was offered the role of sole mistress. Perhaps she learned from her sister's example.

Mary Boleyn Carey became Henry VIII's love interest at an unknown date during the 1520s. Some contemporary rumours implied that Mary's children, Katherine and Henry Carey, were fathered by the King, although he never acknowledged them as his own because the legal implication was that they were fathered by Mary's husband, William Carey. It remains unknown how long Henry VIII's liaison with Mary Boleyn lasted or what their mutual feelings were. The

---

[1] Anne Somerset, *Ladies-in-Waiting*, p. 21.

evidence suggests, however, that Mary Boleyn Carey was more than just a passing fancy.

When the imperial ambassador Chapuys arrived in England in 1529, he quickly discovered that the King had a sexual relationship with Anne Boleyn's sister. "I am not sure that Your Majesty will believe what I am about to state", he wrote to his master, Charles V, "people say that it is only the King's evil destiny that impels him, for had he as he asserts, only attended to the voice of conscience, there would have been still greater affinity to contend with in this intended marriage than in that of the Queen, his wife, a fact of which everyone here speaks quite openly."[2]

There is no evidence to suggest that Mary Boleyn Carey was her sister's lady-in-waiting during the early stages of Henry VIII's divorce; it may be that Mary's presence at court at the time gave courtiers cause to question the legality of Anne's impending marriage. The compromising bond of affinity the King shared with Mary was an impediment, and everyone involved in the case was well aware of this fact. Nicolas Sander, author of *The Rise and Growth of the Anglican Schism* published in 1585, claimed that there was an open hostility between the Boleyn sisters, and Mary, out of jealousy, informed the Queen of her affair with Henry VIII:

---

[2] *Calendar of State Papers, Spain*, Volume 4 Part 1, note 232.

"About this time, Mary Boleyn, the elder sister, seeing that Anne was preferred to her, and that she herself was slighted not only by the King but by her sister, went to the Queen, and bade her be of good cheer; for though the King, she said, was in love with her sister, he could never marry her, for the relations of the king with the family were of such a nature as to make a marriage impossible by the laws of the Church. 'The King himself', she said, 'will not deny it, and I will assert it publicly while I live; now, as he may not marry my sister, so neither will he put Your Majesty away.' The Queen thanked her, and replied that all she had to say and do would be said and done under the direction of her lawyers."[3]

Although some elements of truth may be found in Sander's book, it is nevertheless clear that he sought to depict Henry VIII as an immoral man who had broken with the Catholic Church because he lusted after Anne Boleyn. Anne, on the other hand, was portrayed as a depraved woman, and a heretic at that. There is no evidence that Katherine of Aragon knew about Mary Boleyn Carey's sexual relationship with the King, but if she did know about it, she never used this knowledge to her advantage. However, given that Sander's wild assertions that the whole Boleyn family was lecherous—he claimed, for instance, that Anne Boleyn was Henry VIII's own daughter—it is likely that he invented the scene where

---

[3] Nicolas Sander, *The Rise and Growth of the Anglican Schism*, pp. 32-3.

Mary confesses to Katherine of Aragon that she was the royal mistress.

There are, however, some hints that there might have been an element of rivalry between the Boleyn sisters. In November 1530, Anne received £20 from the King to redeem a jewel from Mary; it may be that this piece was given to Mary over the course of her affair with Henry.[4] Later in her life, Mary admitted that "all the world did set so little by me", indicating that she was not always embraced by her family.[5] Yet when Thomas Boleyn refused to support Mary financially after her husband died of the sweating sickness in the summer of 1528, it was Anne who interceded on her sister's behalf with the King.[6]

Despite the growing tensions at court, Henry VIII was eager to marry Anne Boleyn. In July 1531, shortly before Katherine of Aragon was sent away from court, the imperial ambassador reported that Anne was under the impression that her marriage would take place within three or four months and started appointing her royal household.[7] During the Christmas festivities of that year, Katherine of Aragon no longer presided over the court with Henry VIII, although Anne

---

[4] Eric Ives, *The Life and Death of Anne Boleyn*, p. 210.
[5] Mary Anne Everett Wood, *Letters of Royal and Illustrious Ladies*, Vol.2, p. 195.
[6] Alison Weir, *Mary Boleyn*, p. 242.
[7] *Calendar of State Papers*, Spain, Volume 4 Part 2, note 765.

did not occupy the consort's throne either. One of the observers noted that "there was no mirth because the Queen and the ladies were absent".[8] Anne Boleyn was caught up in an anomalous position; she was neither the King's mistress nor yet his wife, although she was lodged in the royal suite and "accompanied by almost as many ladies as if she were Queen".[9]

One of the ladies who served Anne before she became Queen of England was Anne "Nan" Gainsford, who later became the wife of George Zouche. George Wyatt, the first biographer of Anne Boleyn, compiled his work on the Queen relying on information provided by Nan. Described as "a young and fair gentlewoman", Nan Gainsford was Anne Boleyn's favourite.[10] It was Nan to whom Anne Boleyn lent the proscribed copy of *The Obedience of a Christian Man* by William Tyndale. She also witnessed Anne Boleyn's reaction to a "book of prophecy" found in her chamber. When Anne opened the book, she saw "the figure of some personages with the letter 'H' upon one, 'A' upon another, and 'K' upon the third", which "an expounder" interpreted as indicating "certain destruction" if Anne Boleyn married Henry VIII. Anne called for her maid and showed her contents of the book, explaining what an expounder had told her, "this he said is the

---

[8] Giles Tremlett, *Catherine of Aragon*, p. 355.
[9] *Letters and Papers*, Volume 5, note 696.
[10] George Cavendish, *The Life of Cardinal Wolsey*, p. 439.

King, this is the Queen, mourning, weeping and wringing her hands, and this is myself with my head off". "If I thought it true, though he were an emperor, I would not myself marry him with that condition", Nan replied. Anne Boleyn dismissed the book as "a bauble" and added defiantly, "yet I am resolved to have him, whatsoever might become of me".[11]

Because Nan Gainsford married her fiancé, George Zouche, at an unknown date sometime between 1528 and 1533, she is sometimes confused with another lady of the court, Mary Zouche. Mary was an unmarried young girl when she wrote a pitiful letter to her cousin, John Arundel. She bitterly complained about her stepmother, Susan Welby, begging Arundel to save her and her sister from "the greatest thraldom in the world".[12] According to Mary, her stepmother "never loved none of us all, though we did never so much to please her, and causes my lord my father to be worse to us than he would be, and thus we are brought in so great sorrow that we are weary of our lives". Mary knew that she and her sister could escape from their stepmother only if they were admitted as maids of honour at court:

"Wherefore, my good cousin, I pray you to be so good to us to sue to my lord cardinal [Wolsey] for us that it will

---

[11] Ibid., pp. 429-30.
[12] Mary Anne Everett Wood, *Letters of Royal and Illustrious Ladies*, Vol.1, pp. 313-14.

please his grace to speak to the King and to the Queen, that we may do Her Grace service, or my lady Princess; and we shall pray for his grace the term of our lives, by the grace of God."[13]

Considering that Henry VIII was in love with Anne Boleyn at the time, and she needed as many female supporters as she could get, it is highly possible that Mary Zouche became Anne's maid of honour. The "Mrs Zouche" referred to in Henry VIII's New Year's gifts in 1534 was certainly Mary Zouche; we may assume that she joined Anne Boleyn's household prior to this date, possibly shortly after writing a letter to John Arundel. Mary retained her position in the household of Jane Seymour.[14]

In 1532, Henry VIII ennobled Anne Boleyn, investing her with the title of Marchioness of Pembroke, and took her to the meeting with King Francis I in Calais, where she was presented as Henry's future wife. Although Anne was making diligent preparations for herself and her train of ladies, none of the French noblewomen were there in Calais to greet Anne because she was deemed the King's mistress. Some twenty ladies accompanied Anne to Calais. From this group, she selected six good-looking damsels who danced for Francis I during a banquet on 27 October 1532.

---

[13] Ibid.
[14] *Letters and Papers*, Volume 7, note 9.

Chapter 9:
Anne the Queen, 1533-36

Henry VIII finally married Anne Boleyn in a secret ceremony held at Whitehall Palace in late January 1533. There are two different versions of who accompanied the couple on this occasion. According to the imperial ambassador, Anne's "father, mother, brother and two of her favourites" were present.[1] Later sources stated that Anne Savage was Anne's attendant and bore her train.[2] Mistress Savage was related by marriage to another of Anne Boleyn's ladies-in-waiting, Elizabeth Browne Somerset, Countess of Worcester, and came from a family with a long-standing loyalty to the Tudor dynasty. In April 1533, Anne Savage married Lord Berkeley and retired from court. Her husband died in September 1534 when she was with child; the boy was named after Henry VIII, who stood as his godfather.[3]

In March 1533, Anne Boleyn's royal household had been appointed, although her marriage to the King was still kept secret.[4] Henry VIII ended the speculation on 12 April

---

[1] *Letters and Papers*, Volume 6, note 180.
[2] David Starkey, *Six Wives*, p. 475.
[3] Barbara J. Harris, *The View of My Lady's Chamber*, p. 217.
[4] *Calendar of State Papers, Spain*, Volume 4 Part 2, note 1057.

when he flaunted Anne Boleyn as Queen before the entire court. Clad in cloth of gold and "loaded with the richest jewels", Anne was accompanied by sixty maids of honour and ceremonially led to mass. Her long train was carried by her first cousin, Mary Howard, daughter of the Duke of Norfolk.[5]

The fourteen-year-old Mary Howard had been Anne Boleyn's maid of honour since Anne's ennoblement as Marchioness of Pembroke in September 1532. Anne took special interest in her young cousin, fully aware that Mary might be a useful ally in the near future. Anne had arranged a splendid match between Mary and the King's illegitimate son, Henry Fitzroy, Duke of Richmond, although Mary's mother was against it.

Elizabeth Stafford Howard, Duchess of Norfolk, was Anne Boleyn's aunt by marriage and strongly disliked Anne Boleyn. She had once bluntly told Katherine of Aragon, whom she was very devoted to, that Anne would one day "be the ruin of all her family".[6] Anne was not prepared to tolerate her aunt's outbursts and promptly dismissed her from court.[7] The Duchess of Norfolk's strong dislike of Anne Boleyn may be explained by two factors. First, she prided herself in her Stafford blood—she was daughter of the executed Duke of

---

[5] *Calendar of State Papers, Venice*, Volume 4, note 870.
[6] *Letters and Papers*, Volume 5, note 216.
[7] Ibid., note 238.

Buckingham—and was incensed to see Anne Boleyn, a mere knight's daughter, taking precedence over her.

Although not strictly speaking a commoner—Anne Boleyn was descended from dukes of Norfolk and earls of Ormond—at the time of her meteoric rise to power, her father was only a knighted diplomat and ambassador. He was later created Earl of Wiltshire and Ormond, but Elizabeth Stafford Howard never stopped ridiculing the Boleyns and their origin.[8]

The other reason the Duchess of Norfolk had taken such a strong stance against Anne Boleyn was the fact that Anne had appointed the Duke of Norfolk's mistress as her maid of honour. Bess Holland was derogatorily described by the proud duchess as "a churl's daughter . . . of no gentle blood" and "that harlot which hath put me to all this trouble".[9] Bess was a "young lady" in Anne's service in September 1533 and retained her position in the household of Henry VIII's third wife, Jane Seymour.[10]

According to Anne Boleyn's chaplain, William Latymer, shortly after her coronation, Anne addressed a speech to the officials and chaplains of her household, ordering them to be

---

[8] Paul Friedmann, *Anne Boleyn*, Volume 1, p. 128.
[9] Mary Anne Everett Wood, *Letters of Royal and Illustrous Ladies*, Vol.2, p. 366, 371.
[10] *Letters and Papers*, Volume 6, note 1164.

beyond reproach. She addressed her female staff in a similar vein:

"And that her ladies, maids of honour and other gentlewomen should use themselves according to their calling, Her Grace would . . . commonly and generally many times move them to modesty and chastity; but in especial her maids of honour, whom she would call before her in the Privy Chamber, and before the Mother of Maids would give them a long charge of their behaviours."[11]

Latymer also mentioned an incident when Anne chided one of her maids of honour, her cousin Mary "Madge" Shelton, for scribbling "idle poesies" in her prayer book. The Queen "wonderfully rebuked" Madge for permitting such "wanton toys in her book of prayers" which she termed "mirror or glass wherein she might learn to address her wandering thoughts".[12]

Although this anecdote of the scandalized Queen seems rather ironic considering that during their courtship Anne Boleyn and Henry VIII exchanged love notes on the pages of Anne's book of prayers, it rings true because Madge Shelton's fondness for poetry is well documented. A volume of

---

[11] *William Latymer's Cronickille of Anne Bulleyne*, Volume 39 of Camden Fourth Series, p. 48.
[12] Ibid., p. 63.

poems known as the Devonshire Manuscript survives in the British Library. It contains a large amount of original and transcribed verses. The poems are associated with three of Anne Boleyn's servants: Madge Shelton, Mary Howard and Margaret Douglas. Their initials as well as transcribed poems are found inside the manuscript.

Maria Dowling, editor of William Latymer's *Cronickille of Anne Bulleyne,* acknowledged that Latymer "was anxious to rescue her [Anne's] memory from obloquy", and therefore he was "selective in the material he presents, and the picture he draws is determinedly one-sided".[13] Dowling emphasises that the Anne from Latymer's chronicle "is never shown enjoying music, dancing, feasting or other courtly pleasures" and never delights in the poetry of her brother George, Lord Rochford, or Thomas Wyatt.

That is not to say, of course, that Anne was not as concerned with her maids' moral well-being as Latymer described. According to the teachings of the day, reading scriptures was the best way to prevent young girls from succumbing to fleshly temptations and wasting their precious time on idle pursuits. It lay in Anne's interest to set a high moral standard at her court because she was aware that she had set a dangerous precedent; if she could supplant the

---

[13] Ibid., p. 30.

previous Queen, certainly one of her ladies could topple her. Setting strict rules and directing her ladies' attention to religious activities, such as reading the Bible, attending daily masses and sewing garments for the poor, could certainly help to keep them in check and give the lie to the disparaging of Anne's reputation during Henry VIII's divorce. Anne's silkwoman later claimed that "there was never better order among the ladies and gentlewomen of the court than in Anne Boleyn's day".

Anne Boleyn certainly cared about her maids' reputations. When she was informed[14] that Henry Norris, who was engaged to her cousin Madge Shelton, admired her, Anne confronted Norris and asked him "why he went not through with his marriage?" He replied that "he would tarry a time", angering the Queen. She had spoken back; "you look for a dead man's shoes, for if aught came to the King but good, you would look to have me." Norris was horrified because imagining the King's death was punishable by death. "If he should have any such thought", he said, "he would his head were off". Anne informed him that "she could undo him if she would". This reckless exchange was later blown out of proportion and used against both Anne and Norris. They had been accused of

---

[14] Anne later recalled that it was Francis Weston who told her that "Norris came more unto her chamber for her than for Madge Shelton".

having an affair and plotting the King's death, for which they were executed in May 1536.

"Pastime in the Queen's chamber"

Yet the life of Anne Boleyn's ladies was not all dullness. There was dancing, poetry, singing and gambling. In a letter to Anne's brother, her vice-chamberlain described the goings-on in the Queen's household following her coronation: "as for pastime in the Queen's chamber was never more".[15] Anne's musical abilities, her passion for courtly revels and dancing were later used to support the claim that she was a frivolous hoyden who was guilty of multiple adultery and incest.

Anne Boleyn played in the game of courtly love with enthusiasm, and she was often the focus of amorous poetry and songs. She played the role of unattainable mistress and muse of love-stricken gallants who sought her patronage and approval through sonnets, ballads and praises of her beauty. It was, however, important not to cross the generally accepted boundaries. Historian Greg Walker argued that Anne fell from grace "not as a result of what she did, but of what she said during the May Day weekend of 1536, in a series of incautious conversations with the men who were to be tried and

---

[15] *Letters and Papers*, Volume 6, note 613.

executed with her." In other words: she was unable to draw a line between innocent flirtations within the convention of courtly love and conversations bordering on treason.[16]

It seems that the ladies of Anne Boleyn's household were equally eager players when it came to courtly love. Mary Howard, Duchess of Richmond, was suspected to be "too free with her favours" while her friend, Madge Shelton, became Henry VIII's mistress at some point in 1535.[17] Madge Shelton was beautiful, and Henry VIII's ambassador later observed that Christina of Denmark, whom the King wished to marry, "resembles one Mistress Shelton that used to wait on Queen Anne".[18]

Her good looks and vivacious personality earned Madge many admirers, for Henry Norris was not the only man who fancied her. Francis Weston was rebuked by Anne Boleyn "because he did love her kinswoman Mrs Shelton and . . . he loved not his wife". Weston's response was fashioned after the manner of courtly love. "He loved one in her house better than them both", he replied. When Anne asked "who is that" he used the opportunity to flatter her and replied: "it is yourself". Unfortunately for Weston, Anne recalled this conversation in

[16] Greg Walker, *Rethinking the Fall of Anne Boleyn*, p. 29.
[17] *Chronicle of King Henry VIII (The Spanish Chronicle)*, p. 142.
[18] *Letters and Papers*, Volume 12 Part 2, note 1187.

the Tower and, unintentionally, incriminated him. He was accused of being her lover and executed as a traitor.

The gaiety of Anne Boleyn's court encouraged innocent flirtations to flourish into something more. Margaret Douglas, daughter of Henry VIII's sister, Margaret, Queen of Scots, had served as Anne Boleyn's maid of honour since 1533 and shared close friendships with Mary Howard and Madge Shelton. Margaret fell in love with Lord Thomas Howard, the Duke of Norfolk's half brother, and the couple became secretly engaged on 16 April 1536.[19] Anne Boleyn's sudden arrest and execution on grounds of adultery, incest and treason rendered her daughter, Elizabeth, illegitimate. The new Act of Succession proclaimed Elizabeth an illegitimate daughter of Henry VIII and declared her unfit to be his heiress. Margaret Douglas suddenly became a potential heiress to the throne, at least until the King's new wife provided him with a son.

Shortly afterwards, in July 1536, Margaret's secret betrothal came to light and displeased the King, who believed Lord Howard wanted to usurp the throne through his niece. Servants of Anne Boleyn's household were examined in relation to this matter, yielding evidence of goings-on in the Queen's household. One Thomas Smith revealed that Lord

---

[19] David M. Head, *The Attainder of Lord Thomas Howard and the Tudor Law of Treason,* p.6.

Howard would wait until Lady Boleyn, the Queen's aunt, was gone from Margaret Douglas's chamber, leaving only Mary Howard to attend her before the secret meeting. The couple was arrested and placed in the Tower; Margaret Douglas was eventually sent to live at Syon Abbey and later regained her freedom, but Lord Howard was imprisoned until his death on 31 October 1537.

The King's mistresses in Anne's household

Despite the fact that Henry VIII always ardently proclaimed his love for Anne Boleyn, he returned to his old ways of pursuing new amours soon after the wedding. He took a mistress in the summer of 1533 when Anne was pregnant, incurring the Queen's wrath. When she violently protested, the King replied that she should "shut her eyes and endure" just like Katherine of Aragon did before her.[20]

After Princess Elizabeth's birth, however, Anne resumed her role as Henry's bedfellow and conceived another child. Unfortunately, her pregnancy ended in the summer of 1534. What happened is a matter of conjecture as primary sources are inconclusive. The imperial ambassador remarked that Henry VIII had "begun to entertain doubts as to [Anne's]

---

[20] *Calendar of State Papers, Spain*, Volume 4 Part 2, note 1123.

reported pregnancy", and some scholars have suggested that Anne suffered from pseudocyesis, or a phantom pregnancy.[21] Whatever the outcome of this pregnancy, the King was disappointed with Anne and "has renewed and increased the love which he formerly bore to another very handsome young lady of this court".[22]

This time, however, Anne decided to fight back and enlisted the help of her sister-in-law, Jane Parker Boleyn, known as Lady Rochford. From Chapuys, we know that Henry VIII's elusive mistress, whose identity remains unknown to this day, was one of Anne Boleyn's ladies because the Queen "attempted to dismiss the damsel from her service".[23] How Anne envisaged getting rid of her rival remains unclear, with Chapuys speculating that it was to be done "through quarrelling or otherwise".[24] When the King found out about this conspiracy, he banished Lady Rochford from court and sent his wife a chilling message: "she ought to be satisfied with what he had done for her, for, were he to commence again, he would certainly not do as much".[25] Fortunately for Anne, Henry's fascination with his new mistress quickly faded away,

---

[21] *Calendar of State Papers, Spain*, Volume 5 Part 1, note 90.
John Dewhurst, *The Alleged Miscarriages of Catherine of Aragon and Anne Boleyn*, pp. 49–56.
[22] *Calendar of State Papers, Spain*, Volume 5 Part 1, note 90.
[23] Ibid.
[24] Ibid., note 97.
[25] Ibid., note 90.

but it was only a matter of time before a new lady would try to win the King's heart.

Henry VIII reverted to his pattern of taking a mistress during his wife's pregnancies. When Anne Boleyn was pregnant again in late 1535, the King pursued one of her maids of honour, Jane Seymour. Jane was a seasoned maid of honour who started her career at an unknown date as Katherine of Aragon's servant and later transferred to Anne Boleyn's household. At first, Jane allowed the King to court her in private, but this was soon to change. When Anne accidentally walked in on Jane Seymour sitting on the King's knee, "she for anger and disdain miscarried".[26] Another source adds that Anne lashed out at the King, saying, "I saw this harlot Jane sitting on your knees while my belly was doing its duty!"[27] When Henry VIII confronted her after the miscarriage, Anne claimed that her heart had been broken when she saw the King pursuing other women, a statement that "much grieved" him.[28] Nevertheless, Henry VIII was not about to allow Anne to shift the blame for her miscarriage on him and coolly declared, "I will speak to you when you are well".[29]

---

[26] Henry Clifford, *The Life of the Duchess of Feria*, p. 79.

[27] Eric Ives, *The Life and Death of Anne Boleyn*, p. 304.

[28] *Letters and Papers*, Volume 10, note 351.

[29] Ibid.

Henry VIII started to entertain doubts about his marriage to Anne Boleyn, and the Queen's enemies quickly noticed it. Jane began refusing to see the King in private, and when he sent her a purse full of money with a letter, she threw herself on her knees before the messenger. The implication was that Henry VIII wanted to offer Jane the position of his mistress and paid her in advance. What the King was not aware of was the fact that Jane had been coached by cunning members of the anti-Boleyn faction. She was encouraged to play the old trick on Henry VIII and not yield to his passions unless he offered to marry her. Everyone knew that this tactic worked for Anne Boleyn, and they hoped it would work for Jane as well. The King now courted Jane in the company of chaperones, meeting her in the rooms formerly belonging to Thomas Cromwell, where he installed Jane's elder brother, Edward, and his wife, Anne Stanhope Seymour. Henry could access the room "through certain galleries" without being seen by anyone and pay Jane honourable visits.[30]

In May 1536, the storm of allegations against Queen Anne Boleyn broke over the court. She was accused of plotting the King's death, adultery and incest with her brother. What exactly happened remains one of the most enduring mysteries of Henry VIII's reign. Anne was certainly innocent, as there were no witnesses to her alleged infidelities, and she always

---

[30] *Calendar of State Papers, Spain*, Volume 5 Part 2, note 43.

asserted her innocence, but who exactly brought about her destruction remains an unsolved mystery. Some historians claim that it was Thomas Cromwell, who feared Anne's influence and who decided to get rid of her. Others, however, point out that Anne was not as influential as she used to be and that the King wanted to marry Jane Seymour and was the prime mover against his wife, with Cromwell only fulfilling his orders. Many more allow the possibility that it was the rough edge of Anne's tongue and her flirtatious nature which sent her to the scaffold, while the minority believes that Anne was guilty as charged. Whatever we choose to believe, however, one thing remains certain: Thomas Cromwell, who constructed the case against Anne, claimed that ladies of the Queen's Privy Chamber came forward with damning accusations.

Chapter 10:

Ladies of the Privy Chamber and the fall of Anne Boleyn

On 14 May 1536, Thomas Cromwell wrote to the King's ambassadors in Paris that "the Queen's incontinent living was so rank and common that the ladies of her Privy Chamber could not conceal it". The investigation was sparked off by information concerning Anne Boleyn's offences which "came to the ears" of Henry VIII's councillors, who reported it to the King. "Certain persons of the Privy Chamber and others of her [Anne Boleyn's] side were examined", Cromwell continued, and then it turned out that "the matter was so evident" that the arrests followed immediately. Cromwell had no doubt that Anne Boleyn and her brother would be condemned to death, just as Norris, Weston, Brereton and Smeaton had been two days earlier.[1] He made no mention about the identity of the ladies of Anne's Privy Chamber who accused her, and when Stephen Gardiner expressed "great desire of news", Cromwell replied:

---

[1] *Letters and Papers*, Henry VIII, Volume 10, note 873.

"I wrote as much as plainly of the matters that chanced here as I could devise, unless I should send you the very confessions, which were so abominable that a great part of them were never given in evidence but kept secret".[2]

Cromwell, however, was hiding one very important detail: there were no confessions to send. Shortly after Anne Boleyn's arrest, her vice-chamberlain, Edward Baynton, wrote that no man will "confess" anything against her except Mark Smeaton, indicating that there were serious problems when it came to collecting the evidence. The imperial ambassador, Eustace Chapuys, who reported invaluable details from the trials, corroborated this version and wrote that only Mark Smeaton confessed to having had carnal knowledge of the Queen, but others, including Anne herself, were "sentenced on mere presumption or on very slight grounds, without legal proof or valid confession".[3]

Confessions

Edward Baynton was tasked to extract confessions from members of Anne Boleyn's household, as implied by Thomas Cromwell, but he came across certain difficulties.

---

[2] Muriel St Clare Byrne, *The Lisle Letters*, Vol.3, p. 375.
[3] *Calendar of State Papers, Spain,* Volume 5 Part 2, note 55.

Margery Horsman, one of Anne's maids of honour, "had used herself strangely towards me of late", Baynton reported and assumed that it was because "there has lately been great friendship between the Queen and her".[4]

Another lady who was certainly examined was Jane Parker Boleyn, Lady Rochford, Anne Boleyn's sister-in-law. Lady Rochford has come down in history as the "wicked wife, accuser of her own husband."[5] However, the contemporary accounts do not name Lady Rochford as the star witness, and she only appears in the context of a mysterious piece of paper with Anne's statement about the King's sexual prowess. The imperial ambassador reported that Anne confided in her sister-in-law that the King was impotent and had "neither the skill nor the virility to satisfy a woman".

This accusation was put to George Boleyn in writing, but he was forbidden to read it aloud. George, however, did read it aloud, saying that he couldn't possibly speculate for fear of arousing suspicion which might prejudice Henry VIII's issue.[6] He was defending himself so eloquently that odds ran ten to one for an acquittal, according to Chapuys.[7] George Constantine, one of Henry Norris's servants, later wrote that

---

[4] *Letters and Papers*, Volume 10, note 799.
[5] George Cavendish, *The Life and Death of Cardinal Wolsey*, p.446.
[6] *Letters and Papers*, Volume 10, note 908.
[7] Ibid.

he had heard that George would have escaped death "had it not been for a letter", the same letter, presumably, containing his wife's confession, which he had read aloud.[8]

The other possibility, raised in the 1576 edition of John Foxe's *Acts and Monuments*, states that "it is reported of some that this Lady Rochford forged a false letter against her husband and Queen Anne her sister, by the which they were both cast away".[9] The idea of a letter appeared also in Alexander Ales's letter of congratulation sent to Queen Elizabeth I on her accession. Ales, who was present at court at the time of Anne Boleyn's downfall, picked up a story that certain letters, in which Anne informed George that she was pregnant, were produced at her trial as proof of their incest.[10]

If there was indeed a letter of some sort written or delivered by Lady Rochford, we may never learn its contents since, as the seventeenth-century historian Gilbert Burnet observed, most of the records of interrogations were deliberately destroyed. Burnet had access to the trial sources lost to us, and he reached the conclusion that Lady Rochford was a "spiteful wife" who was jealous of her husband's relationship with Anne Boleyn and "carried many stories to the King, or some about him, to persuade that there was a

---

[8] Elizabeth Norton, *Anne Boleyn in Her Own Words*, p. 205.
[9] John Foxe, *The Acts and Monuments*, Vol. 5., p. 462.
[10] *Calendar of State Papers Foreign*, Elizabethan, Volume 1, note 1303.

familiarity between the Queen and her brother, beyond what so near a relation could justify".[11]

Burnet's opinion of Lady Rochford, however, was heavily influenced by her involvement in Queen Katherine Howard's affair with Thomas Culpeper.[12] As we will see later in the book, Lady Rochford helped to arrange meetings between the young Queen and Culpeper, and was executed for her involvement in 1542.

In her recent biography of Lady Rochford, historian Julia Fox dispelled the myth that Jane Parker Boleyn had given false testimony of Anne Boleyn's incest with George. She tracked down the development of the myth and argued that Jane had become history's "perfect scapegoat" because, during the reign of Anne Boleyn's daughter, the explanation was needed as to why the Queen was falsely accused and executed. The blame could not have been shifted to Henry VIII, from whom Queen Elizabeth derived her claim to the throne, so it has been suggested that someone fed him lies about Anne Boleyn's misconduct. That someone was Jane Parker Boleyn,

---

[11] Gilbert Burnet, *The History of the Reformation of the Church of England*, Vol.1, p. 146.
[12] Ibid.

who had no one to speak up for her and was executed for her role in Katherine Howard's extramarital affair.[13]

However, not all historians agree that Lady Rochford should be wholly extricated from her involvement in Anne Boleyn's downfall. Muriel St Clare Byrne, the editor of *The Lisle Letters*, noticed that Lady Rochford "had in some way earned the gratitude of the Queen's accusers" because her father-in-law, Thomas Boleyn, received orders from Henry VIII and Thomas Cromwell to augment her living to £100 a year instead of the humble 100 marks she had been previously allowed.[14] Historians Margery S. Schauer and Frederick Schauer pointed out that while there was an implication that George Boleyn was charged with knowing about his sister's confession regarding the King's sexual prowess, he was guilty of misprision of treason—knowing about treasonous activity and not reporting it to the authorities. But if George was guilty of misprision of treason, so was his wife, and yet Lady Rochford was neither charged nor executed.[15]

However, there is also evidence to suggest that Jane Parker Boleyn was the only person who had promised her husband to intercede with the King on his behalf. In her letter

---

[13] http://www.juliafox.co.uk/A-talk-with-Julia-Fox.pdf
[14] Muriel St Clare Byrne, *The Lisle Letters*, Vol.3, pp. 380-1.
[15] Margery S. Schauer and Frederick Schauer, *Law as the Engine of State: The Trial of Anne Boleyn*, 22 Wm. & Mary L. Rev. 49 (1980).

to George Boleyn, written two days after his arrest, Jane promised "to humbly [make] suit unto the King's highness", although historian Eric Ives believed that "we may, if we choose, smell malice, for the message was brought with Henry's express permission and by Carew and Bryan in his newly turned coat".[16] Nicholas Carew and Francis Bryan were kin to Anne and George Boleyn, but they both worked to their utter destruction and coached Jane Seymour to supplant Anne.

Although the evidence concerning Lady Rochford's involvement in Anne Boleyn's fall allows us to speculate about the extent of her involvement, there are some indications that she grieved after her husband's death. The notion that George and Jane's marriage was an unhappy union because of George's alleged homosexuality, a theory put forward by Retha M. Warnicke, has been disproved by other historians due to the lack of convincing evidence.[17] As to the nature of the relationship between the couple, there is no evidence that would help us reach a convincing conclusion about their marital life.

One of Jane's contemporaries described her as a "widow in black", suggesting that she appeared as a grieving

---

[16] Eric Ives, *The Life and Death of Anne Boleyn*, p. 332.
[17] Ibid.

widow in the public eye after George's death.[18] The inventories carried out after her execution in 1542 tally with this description and reveal that Lady Rochford owned gowns, kirtles and sleeves of black damasks, satins and velvets.[19]

"First accuser"

In a letter written by John Husee, the London agent of the Lisle family, he revealed what he was able to gather from his acquaintances at court:

"And touching the confession of the Queen and the others, they said little or nothing. But what was said was wondrous discreetly spoken: the first accusers, the Lady Worcester, and Nan Cobham, with one maid more. But the Lady Worcester was the first ground . . ."[20]

He was apparently confident about the identity of Anne Boleyn's accusers, and in his next letter, he confirmed that "my Lady Worcester beareth name to be the principal".[21] The Lady Worcester mentioned here was Elizabeth Browne Somerset, Countess of Worcester. She was Anne Boleyn's lady-in-waiting and a close friend. Anne had lent her £100, a

---

[18] Elizabeth Norton, *The Boleyn Women*, p. 193.
[19] Ibid.
[20] Muriel St Clare Byrne, *The Lisle Letters*, Vol.3, pp. 378.
[21] Ibid.

substantial sum she borrowed from the Queen without her husband's knowledge. Their friendship dates to the time before Anne became Queen; the Privy Purse expenses for February 1530 reveal "reward to the nurse and midwife of my Lady of Worcester".[22] Shortly after her arrival to the Tower, Anne "much lamented my Lady of Worcester" because "her child did not stir in her body . . . for the sorrow she took for me".[23] This emotional outpouring proves just how close a friend Anne believed the Countess of Worcester was.

What did the Countess of Worcester confess? The question would linger unanswered had it not been for a poem describing Anne Boleyn's downfall written in French on 2 June 1536 by Lancelot de Carles, who then served the French ambassador at the English court. *A Letter Containing the Criminal Charges Laid Against Queen Anne Boleyn of England* was first printed in Lyons in 1545. This piece of evidence is remarkably accurate when it comes to well-known facts of Anne Boleyn's life, but it is also very controversial since it details how and in what circumstances one of the Queen's ladies-in-waiting revealed the strange goings-on in Anne Boleyn's chambers.

---

[22] *Letters and Papers*, Volume 5, f. 13.
[23] *Letters and Papers*, Volume 10, note 793.

The poem says that when one member of the Privy Council rebuked his sister for her loose living, she retorted that the Queen was far worse because she entertained gentlemen in her private chambers at undue hours and had sexual relationships with her own brother and the courtly musician, Mark Smeaton. The councillor was now in a dangerous position, and if the Queen's behaviour came to light, he would suffer penalty for misprision of treason. He confided the news to the King's closest advisors, so the poem tells us, and that is how the investigation into Anne Boleyn's conduct started. Historian Muriel St Clare Byrne identified the scolded lady as Elizabeth Browne Somerset, Countess of Worcester, and her brother as Anthony Browne.[24]

The version of events described in the poem confirms what Thomas Cromwell wrote in his letter of 14 May 1536 and tallies with John Husee's two letters in which he identified Anne's first accuser as the Countess of Worcester. However, a fragmentary note made by Judge John Spelman, who presided over the trials of Anne Boleyn's alleged lovers, reveals that the matter of the Queen's lax morals was "disclosed by a woman called the Lady Wingfield, who was a servant of the said Queen and shared the same tendencies".[25]

---

[24] Muriel St Clare Byrne, *The Lisle Letters*, Vol. 3, p. 379.
[25] Eric Ives, *The Life and Death of Anne Boleyn*, p. 329.

According to Spelman, this lady revealed what she knew about Anne Boleyn's allegedly loose living on her deathbed. Lady Wingfield died in 1534, so she was not personally interrogated or confronted with Anne Boleyn's crimes. Unfortunately, the statement is incomplete, and the whole story of how the Lady Wingfield revealed Anne Boleyn's misconduct, and who informed the authorities of it, remains unknown. However, there is no mention of the Countess of Worcester. It is highly unlikely that Spelman got it wrong and instead of "Worcester" scribbled "Wingfield", especially since Lady Wingfield was known to have been Anne Boleyn's former lady-in-waiting.

Bridget Wiltshire, Lady Wingfield, lived in Stone Castle, close to Anne's family home at Hever. Anne had been on good terms with Bridget's second husband, Nicholas Harvey, who served as an ambassador at the court of the Holy Roman Emperor and, according to Eustace Chapuys, was Anne's "strong partisan".[26] Chapuys, as the Holy Roman Emperor's ambassador in England, took an interest in Harvey and his wife, reporting that Bridget came to court in attendance on Anne Boleyn in June 1530.[27]

---

[26] *Calendar of State Papers, Spain*, Volume 4 Part 1, note 345.
[27] Ibid.

A tantalizing letter written by Anne Boleyn to this lady reveals that they shared a close relationship, but at the same time, it reveals that the two may have shared a secret. Anne claimed that, next to her own mother, there was no other woman whom she loved better than Lady Wingfield, but she urged her to leave her "indiscreet trouble, both for displeasing of God and also for displeasing of me, that doth love you so entirely".[28] This "indiscreet trouble" mentioned by Anne Boleyn in her letter to Lady Wingfield will forever remain a mystery, although the implication is that Lady Wingfield's close relationship to Anne Boleyn imparted an air of credibility to her deathbed confession.

Accomplices

When the news of Anne Boleyn's arrest spread like wildfire round the country, it was rumoured that "sundry ladies" were thrown into the Tower as Anne's accomplices.[29] As later events have shown, however, it turned out that only the Queen and her alleged lovers were imprisoned. Curiously, none of Anne Boleyn's ladies-in-waiting were executed with her. Lady Wingfield was conveniently dead, and whoever

---

[28] Eric Ives, *The Life and Death of Anne Boleyn*, p. 330.
[29] *Letters and Papers*, Volume 10, note 785.

informed the authorities about her deathbed confession was, surprisingly, not accused of misprision of treason.

The only source that claims that one of Anne Boleyn's ladies was executed is *The Spanish Chronicle*. According to this dubious source, Anne Boleyn had an old woman in her service named Margaret, who was arranging meetings between Anne and her lovers. The chronicle goes on to say that the councillors who interrogated the men accused as Anne Boleyn's lovers had "put old Margaret to the torture, who told the whole story of how she had arranged that Mark and Master Norris and Brereton should all have access to the Queen unknown to each other". Armed with Margaret's confession, "the gentlemen ordered the old woman to be burnt that night within the Tower, and they took her confession to the King; and the King ordered all the prisoners to be beheaded".[30] The chronicle's next chapter ads a grim twist to this incredible tale:

"We have told how the old woman was ordered to be burned in the great courtyard of the Tower, and they made the Queen see it from an iron-barred window. She said, 'Why do you grieve me so? I wish they would burn me with her', to

---

[30] *Chronicle of King Henry VIII (The Spanish Chronicle)*, p. 66.

which the keeper answered, 'Madam, another death is reserved for you.'"[31]

How reliable is this account? Many stories related by *The Spanish Chronicle,* including this one, are not corroborated by other contemporary sources, and the chronology is off in many places. The chronicle has, for example, Anne Boleyn visiting Calais after her coronation, while it actually happened many months before she was crowned. Anne's brother is constantly referred to as the "Duke of Somerset", while he never held such a title. Errors and incorrect chronology are part of *The Spanish Chronicle,* and therefore the story of the old Margaret burned at the stake within the Tower as Anne Boleyn's accomplice must be taken with a touch of reserve.

But Anne Boleyn wasn't alone in the Tower of London. "I think much unkindness in the King to put such about me as I never loved", she bitterly complained to William Kingston. Kingston, whose wife was one of the ladies who attended to Anne's daily needs in the Tower, replied that "the King took them to be honest and good women". But Anne insisted that "I would have had of my own Privy Chamber which I favour most".[32] Indeed, none of the four women who accompanied Anne sympathised with her; quite the contrary, they had been appointed to spy on her. Anne especially resented her aunt,

---

[31] Ibid., p. 67.
[32] *Letters and Papers*, Volume 10, note 797.

Lady Anne Tempest Boleyn, and Margaret Dymoke, Lady Coffin, "for they could tell her nothing of my lord her father nor nothing else, but she defied them all".[33]

Ladies Boleyn and Coffin were allocated to sleep on a pallet bed in the Queen's bedchamber while William Kingston and his wife slept outside the door. Kingston reported to Thomas Cromwell that "I have everything told me by Mistress Coffin that she thinks meet for me to know".[34] Coffin might have been the same lady who also spied for the imperial ambassador, Eustace Chapuys:

"The lady who had charge of her [Anne] has sent to tell me in great secrecy that the Concubine, before and after receiving the sacrament, affirmed to her, on the damnation of her soul, that she had never been unfaithful to the King."[35]

Reaction and aftermath

Although Anne Boleyn hoped that her life would be spared and believed that Henry VIII was only testing her, her royal household was disbanded before she was even tried:

---

[33] Ibid., 798.
[34] Ibid., note 793.
[35] Ibid., note 908.

"And the morrow after, being Saturday, and the thirteenth day of May, Master FitzWilliam, Treasurer of the King's household, and Mr Controller, deposed and broke up the Queen's household at Greenwich, and so discharged all of her servants of their offices clear."[36]

On 19 May 1536, the day of Anne's execution, it was well known that the Queen's servants received permission to seek employment elsewhere and that the King, "of his goodness", had retained some of them.[37] Indeed, many members of Anne's household, including all of the ladies who were linked to her downfall, smoothly transferred to the new Queen's establishment.

What did Anne Boleyn's ladies-in-waiting think about their executed Queen? Did they believe she was guilty? Some clue is offered by Alexander Ales, who had picked up a rumour that Anne Boleyn's ladies-in-waiting were offered bribes to testify against their Queen.[38] This means that at least some of them were reluctant to testify against Anne.

Although Anne Boleyn feared for the Countess of Worcester's unborn child's life, Elizabeth Browne Somerset gave birth to a healthy baby girl whom she named, perhaps in

---

[36] Charles Wriothesley, *A Chronicle of England During the Reigns of the Tudors*, Vol. 1, p. 37.
[37] Muriel St Clare Byrne, *The Lisle Letters*, Vol. 4, p. 48.
[38] *Calendar of State Papers Foreign*, Elizabethan, Volume 1, note 1303.

memory of the Queen, Anne.[39] Margery Horsman,[40] who was reluctant to testify against Anne Boleyn, transferred to Jane Seymour's household, becoming one of her favourite attendants and the keeper of the Queen's jewels, money and other treasures.[41] "Nan Cobham" and "one maid more" whose testimonials were so useful to the government, were never satisfactorily identified.[42]

One lady who retained good memories of the Queen was her first cousin, Mary Howard, Duchess of Richmond. After Anne Boleyn's execution and the death of her husband, Henry Fitzroy, in July 1536, Mary retired from court to her father's estates at Kenninghall and did not join the household of Jane Seymour. Years later, when she was raising her executed brother's children, she became a patroness of the Protestant John Fox, author of *The Acts and Monuments*, the book that charts the origins and progress of the Reformation in England and immortalises those who died for their Protestant beliefs. During Foxe's time in the Duchess of Richmond's household, they often talked about Anne Boleyn. This is what the duchess told Foxe:

---

[39] G.W. Bernard, *Anne Boleyn*, p. 154.

[40] She married Michael Lyster and was henceforward known as Margery Lyster.

[41] *Letters and Papers*, Volume 12 Part 2, note 1150.

[42] Historian Eric Ives proposed that the "one maid more" listed by John Husee as Anne Boleyn's accuser may have been Margery Horsman. [Eric Ives, *The Life and Death of Anne Boleyn*, p. 332.]

"It hath been reported unto us by divers credible persons who were about this Queen, and daily acquainted with her doings, concerning her liberal and bountiful distribution to the poor, how Her Grace carried ever about her a certain little purse, out of which she was wont daily to scatter abroad some alms to the needy, thinking no day well spent wherein some man had not fared the better by some benefit at her hands."[43]

To lend credibility to his description of Anne Boleyn, Foxe added:

"And this I write by the relation of certain noble personages who were the chief and principal of her waiting maids about her, specially the Duchess of Richmond by name."[44]

Mary Howard certainly did not believe lies spread about Anne Boleyn's morals at court. She was, after all, very close to Anne and knew that she couldn't have possibly committed such heinous crimes. Had she believed that her royal mistress was an adulteress, she would never have entertained such a good opinion of her.

There are hints that Anne Boleyn was indeed innocent of the charges laid against her in May 1536. In a rare moment

---

[43] John Foxe, *Acts and Monuments*, Vol. 5, p.63
[44] Ibid.

of honesty, Henry VIII linked Anne Boleyn's death to meddling into politics rather than to multiple counts of adultery. As soon as Jane Seymour seized her opportunity to plead with the King on a matter of utmost political importance, she was brusquely warned, in front of the whole court, "not to meddle" with the King's affairs. Henry VIII mercilessly reminded her of the late Queen's fate. Jane was, as one might imagine, horrified.[45]

---

[45] *Letters and Papers*, Volume 11, note 860.

Chapter 11:

"Many ancient ladies" in Queen Jane Seymour's household

When Henry VIII married Jane Seymour, there was a general feeling that a period of peace and marital bliss had succeeded an era of political instability and unhappiness. As one courtier observed, "the King hath come out of hell into heaven for the gentleness in this [Jane] and the cursedness and the unhappiness in the other [Anne]".[1] Jane Seymour was Queen of England for only one year and four months, and she succeeded where her predecessors had failed, delivering a longed-for male heir in October 1537. Her premature death at the age of twenty-nine after an excruciating labour marked her as Henry VIII's one true love and the mother of his sole surviving legitimate son.

Historians, however, tend to dismiss her as a meek, docile woman and something of a dullard. She is usually regarded as Queen of little interest historically, but the Tudor historiography presents her as an intelligent and calculating young woman who had a clear vision of her queenship. Jane

---

[1] *Letters and Papers*, Volume 10, note 1047.

Seymour knew exactly what Henry VIII wanted in a wife. She may have heard that he complained to several courtiers that Anne Boleyn, unlike Katherine of Aragon, had abused him with ill words on many occasions and had dared to lecture him on matters of religion. She had also refused to turn a blind eye on his relationships with other women and berated him, often in public, for his marital infidelities. Jane decided to become the opposite of her executed predecessor in every possible way.

"Bound to obey and serve"

When William Kingston visited the royal court in January 1536, he observed that "here is much youth".[2] Indeed, both Anne Boleyn and Henry VIII surrounded themselves with young people whose presence invigorated them. When Jane Seymour proceeded to select her female staff, however, she decided to choose matronly ladies-in-waiting rather than young and inexperienced ones. Two days after her servants were sworn in on 4 June 1536, one courtier noticed that "here is a very great and triumphant court, and many ancient ladies and gentlewomen in it".[3]

---

[2] Muriel St Clare Byrne, *The Lisle Letters*, Vol.3, p. 265.
[3] Ibid, Vol.4, p. 196.

The matronly composition of her court and a carefully chosen motto, "bound to obey and serve", invited comparisons to Henry VIII's first wife, Katherine of Aragon. Like Katherine, Jane was a Catholic with pro-imperial sympathies. She made it clear from the outset that she planned to bring about the King's reconciliation with his elder daughter, Mary, who had been degraded to the position of "Lady Mary" after Anne Boleyn gave birth to Elizabeth.

Mary's relationship with Anne Boleyn had been far from ideal. Anne had always been aware that her political enemies had clustered around Mary, and so she sought to diminish the girl's position. In her desperation, Anne had boasted that she would make Mary her maid of honour and force her to marry beneath her station. When Katherine of Aragon died, Anne changed her tactics and promised Mary that "if she wished to come to court, she would be exempted from holding the tail of her gown", but Mary bluntly refused.[4] Now, with Anne dead and the King's new wife planning to reconcile Mary with the King, Mary wrote a letter offering Jane Seymour her service.[5] Mary was, however, forced to recognise her illegitimacy first, and only when she finally signed the document declaring the marriage between her parents as illegal, was she welcomed at court.

---

[4] *Letters and Papers*, Volume 10, note 141.
[5] Ibid., note 1022.

Mistress of the household

Jane Seymour proved to be a difficult mistress to please. First, she ordered all of her ladies to dress in the traditional English apparel instead of flaunting their décolletages and revealing generous amounts of hair in clothes and caps cut in the French fashion. This was a conscious choice of a woman who sought to distance herself from her executed predecessor. Anne Boleyn was brought up in France and excelled in everything French. The King commented that he had "too much experience of French bringing up and manners", signalling that he was tired of Anne's ways.[6] Jane quickly realized this and introduced changes in her household.

Jane's aversion to everything French is best illustrated by her reluctance to admit one of the Lady Lisle's daughters to her household. The young Anne Basset was educated in the French household and this fact was probably very inconvenient for the new Queen. Jane Seymour might have been aware that Lady Lisle had sent her two daughters to be educated in France to appeal to Anne Boleyn's tastes. At some point, Lady Lisle realized that her beautiful daughter Anne would probably never become Jane Seymour's maid of honour

---

[6] *Calendar of State Papers*, *Spain*, Volume 5 Part 2, note 61.

and told her London agent that she "thought the Queen's grace did not favour her", although he begged to differ.[7]

The letters exchanged between the Lisle family and their agents at court provide a unique glimpse into the courtly protocol. John Husee, who did everything he could to help install Anne Basset in the Queen's household, approached many noblewomen who were of some consequence at court. Placing one's daughter in the royal household was a daunting task, and Husee quickly learned that men, even if influential, would not meddle into such womanly matters, and so he approached ladies who stood highly in Jane Seymour's favour. The Countesses of Rutland and Sussex, Ladies Beauchamp and Wallop, as well as Mistresses Coffin and Horsman, proved to be very useful intermediaries.

Thomas Manners, Earl of Rutland, replaced Thomas Burgh as Lord Chamberlain in the Queen's household. The earl's wife, Eleanor Paston Manners, Countess of Rutland, became one of the leading ladies-in-waiting within Jane Seymour's Privy Chamber. The Countess of Rutland was not a newcomer at court; her earliest appearance was recorded at the investiture of Anne Boleyn with the Marquisate of Pembroke in 1532.[8] The countess's husband's position placed her high in the royal favour, and the fact that she was a

---

[7] Muriel St Clare Byrne, *The Lisle Letters*, Vol. 4, p. 155.
[8] *Letters and Papers*, Volume 5, note 1274.

conservative Catholic helped her find a common ground with Jane Seymour. John Husee regarded the Countess of Rutland as an authority on social etiquette and praised her as "one of the greatest ladies and woman of most honour as I ever knew".[9]

Mary Arundel Radcliffe, Countess of Sussex, was Lady Lisle's niece and one of her most important intermediaries at court. She started her service as Jane Seymour's maid of honour and became the Queen's lady-in-waiting after her marriage to Robert Radcliffe, Earl of Sussex, in January 1537. The earl was in his fifties and Mary was in her early twenties at the time of their wedding. Her youth and good looks attracted John Husee's comment: "some are glad of it and some sorry for the gentlewoman's sake."[10] She was described by Lady Wallop as "the fairest and the gentlest lady that I know".[11] Elizabeth Harleston, Lady Wallop, was another very influential lady-in-waiting. Her husband, John Wallop, served as an ambassador to France, and they both accompanied Henry VIII and Anne Boleyn to Calais in 1532, with Lady Wallop dancing beside Anne as one of the six masked ladies.

One of Jane Seymour's favourite ladies-in-waiting was her sister-in-law, Anne Stanhope Seymour. Anne was married

[9] Muriel St Clare Byrne, *The Lisle Letters*, Vol.4, p. 106.
[10] *Letters and Papers*, Volume 12 Part 1, note 86.
[11] Muriel St Clare Byrne, *The Lisle Letters*, Vol.5, p. 196.

to Jane's elder brother, Edward, since about 1535, and the available evidence suggests that Jane was on very good terms with Edward and his wife. In February 1537, for instance, she stood as one of the two godmothers to their first child (the second was Lady Mary). Although there is no firm evidence of when Anne Stanhope Seymour began her career at court, it is possible that she became Katherine of Aragon's maid of honour in the 1520s.[12] In the Queen's household, Anne had forged a lifelong friendship with Katherine's daughter, Mary. Mary never lost affection for Anne Stanhope Seymour despite the fact that their religious views diverged in the late 1530s; Anne became a follower of the New Religion, while Mary remained staunchly Catholic.

Among Jane Seymour's newly appointed maids of honour were Anne Parr and Mary Norris. Anne Parr was a daughter of Maud Green Parr, one of the favourite ladies-in-waiting of Katherine of Aragon. She was also a sister of Katherine Parr, who would become Henry VIII's sixth wife in the years to come. Mary Norris was a daughter of Henry Norris, executed as Anne Boleyn's alleged lover in May 1536. It seems that Norris's daughter was among Jane Seymour's

---

[12] In a letter to Anne, Mary Tudor wrote: "when you were one of Her Grace's [Katherine of Aragon's] maids . . ." (*The Museum of Foreign Literature, Science, and Art, Volumes* 37-38, p. 262.)

favourite servants because she awarded the girl with little trinkets of jewellery.[13]

Jane Seymour was generous to her ladies and often rewarded them for services they rendered her. A list of the Queen's jewels drawn up shortly after her death reveals that she had often presented her favourite female servants with jewels. The Countesses of Rutland and Sussex were given bejewelled girdles (decorative cords worn around the waist). Among the ladies who received "jewels, pomanders and tablets" were Margery Horsman, now styled lady Lyster; Jane Parker Boleyn, Lady Rochford; and the King's daughters, ladies Mary and Elizabeth.[14]

It is noteworthy that Jane Seymour had a younger sister, Elizabeth Seymour, who mostly stayed away from court during her sister's time as Queen. Elizabeth married her first husband, Anthony Ughtred of Kexby, in 1531 and bore him two children. By 1537, she was a young widow living on reduced means in York. Her sister's unexpected marriage to the King raised Elizabeth's chances for a better living and a good match. In March 1537, she wrote a letter to Thomas Cromwell, asking for the grant of some of the goods from one of the dissolved monasteries.

---

[13] *Letters and Papers*, Volume 12 Part 2, note 973.
[14] Ibid.

Elizabeth's letter strongly suggests that she either believed that her sister had no influence with Henry VIII, and the only person who could help her was Cromwell, or that the sisters were on bad terms. "I put mine only trust in your lordship for the good expedition thereof, and intend to sue to none other but only to your lordship", Elizabeth assured Cromwell.[15] Her letter suggests that she visited court on occasion—she reminded Cromwell that "at my last being at the court I desired your lordship that I might be so bold as to be a suitor to you"—but she was not one of her royal sister's regular ladies-in-waiting.[16] Cromwell responded very kindly to Elizabeth's plea and, apparently impressed with her, decided to arrange a marriage between her and his only son and heir, Gregory. As the Queen's sister, Elizabeth was a valuable catch and tying himself to the royal family was a wise move on Cromwell's part. Elizabeth married Gregory Cromwell in August 1537.

Jane Seymour died only two months later, leaving Henry VIII a widower. But the Queen did not die in vain; she died as a result of childbed fever after delivering a son, Prince Edward. Now Thomas Cromwell's son was an uncle of the future King of England.

---

[15] Mary Anne Everett Wood, *Letters of Royal and Illustrious Ladies*, Vol. 2, p. 353-4.
[16] Ibid.

None of Henry VIII's previous wives died as queens, and Jane Seymour's grand funeral mirrored that of the King's mother, Elizabeth of York, who had died in similar circumstances in 1503. The Queen's ladies-in-waiting performed one last duty to their royal mistress, keeping vigils around Jane Seymour's lifeless body, attending numerous masses and wearing "mourning habits". In the early morning of 12 November 1537, the Queen's body was moved from the chapel at Hampton Court to a chariot drawn by six horses. Lady Mary, Jane Seymour's favourite stepdaughter, was the chief mourner and rode on a horse trapped with black velvet. Following her were a number of chariots containing ladies-in-waiting and maids of honour who served in the Queen's household.[17]

---

[17] *Letters and Papers*, Volume 12 Part 2, note 1060.

Chapter 12:

Anne of Cleves's queenly household

After Jane Seymour's death, Henry VIII was reportedly "in good health and merry as a widower may be".[1] Although Jane Seymour became his successful wife and the only one who provided him with a son who would eventually succeed his father on the throne, in October 1537, Henry VIII was faced with a dilemma: Should he remarry? His son, little Edward, was no more than just a toddler in a silver cradle and, although Henry wished the boy to survive infancy, the possibility of his early death was always at the back of the King's mind. It was reasonable to search for another wife and try to beget more sons. Although Henry VIII did not remarry for two years after Jane's death, the talk about such a possibility commenced very shortly after the Queen's demise.

In early 1539, Thomas Cromwell proposed a marriage pact between Henry VIII and one of the two sisters of the Duke of Cleves. Cromwell, knowing fully well that the King had to fall in love with his prospective bride, ordered Christopher

---

[1] *Letters and Papers*, Volume 12 Part 2, note 1023.

Mont, the ambassador who was sent to the Duke of Cleves's court, to inspect "the beauty and qualities of [Anne], the eldest of the two daughters of Cleves, her shape, stature and complexion".[2] The fact that Anne of Cleves came down in history as "the Flanders Mare" has absolutely no basis in what Anne's contemporaries though of her; in fact, she was praised by everyone who had seen her. "Every man", wrote Christopher Mont, "praiseth the beauty of the said Lady, as well for the face, as for the whole body, above all other ladies excellent".[3] When the King saw Anne's portrait, he fell in love with the image and decided to marry her as soon as possible.

Late in 1539, the twenty-four-year-old Anne of Cleves left her homeland and reached Calais. She received a warm welcome there, and although she needed translators to help her communicate with the English delegates, she was eager to learn the ways of her new country. Although Anne arrived with an entourage of her own, the King also established a household for her in advance of her arrival. Henry VIII decided that his new wife should have thirty women who would daily serve her, including Margaret Douglas, his niece, and Mary Howard, his former daughter-in-law.[4] Anne of Cleves's own

---

[2] Starkey, *Six Wives*, p. 617.
[3] Ibid.
[4] John Gough Nichols, *The Chronicle of Calais*, p. 170.

maids of honour made little impression at court. The French ambassador reported that:

"She brings in her suite twelve or fifteen damsels as maids of honour, all dressed in the same fashion and with the same vestments (as to colour and cloth) which she herself wears—a thing which has seemed rather strange in this place".[5]

The damsels were "not only inferior to her [Anne of Cleves] in beauty, but dressed in such coarse and unsightly garb that they would be considered ugly through it even had they any personal attractions".[6] The custom dictated that most of a foreign bride's entourage would be sent home, and this time it happened very quickly after the King's wedding to Anne of Cleves. But not all of Anne's ladies left England. In March 1540, Thomas Cromwell's remembrances included a reference to "the Queen's servants; how the strangers [foreigners] shall be paid that came over with Her Grace".[7] Four months later, a warrant was issued for the payment of wages to the officers of Anne of Cleves's household, including Katherine and Gertrude, Dutch women, who received £10 apiece.[8]

---

[5] *Calendar of State Papers*, *Spain*, Volume 6 Part 1, Preface.

[6] Ibid.

[7] *Letters and Papers*, Volume 15, note 322.

[8] Ibid., note 937.

Among the ladies who stayed in England was Mrs Loew, a German noblewoman who served as the Mother of Maids. She had a great deal of influence over the new Queen, and when Lady Lisle tried to obtain a post of maid of honour for her daughter Katherine Basset, she was advised to approach Mrs Loew. It quickly became apparent, however, that Anne of Cleves was only a nominal head of her new household, and it was the King who decided which ladies should be appointed. When Lord Lisle, Katherine Basset's stepfather, broached the subject of placing her in the Queen's household with the German diplomat, Henry Olisleger, he received a very kind but unpromising reply:

"My lord, very sorry at heart I am to advertise [inform] you that with the knowledge and goodwill of the Queen's Grace I have spoken with the King our master and also with my Lord Privy Seal [Thomas Cromwell] and the other gentlemen of the Council, to have Mistress Katherine, your wife's daughter, to be of the Privy Chamber with the Queen; to the which I have had answer made me that the ladies and gentlewomen of the Privy Chamber were appointed before Her Grace's coming, and that for this time patience must be had. And however much I have earnestly prayed that the gentlewoman might be taken to be of the number of the others as only for the Queen's pleasure, nevertheless I have received the same reply, for the which I am very sorry, and that I cannot at this time advertise you that I have done you pleasure in this your desire".[9]

Katherine Basset's younger sister Anne was the Queen's maid of honour and stood highly in the King's favour, with some historians suggesting that she was a royal mistress. Lady Lisle pestered Anne to intercede with the King on Katherine's behalf, but Anne, too, was powerless:

"And whereas you write to me that I should remember my sister, I have spoken to the King's Highness for her, and His Grace made me answer that Master Bryan and divers others had spoken to His Grace for her friends, but he said he would not grant me nor them as yet; for His Grace said that he would have them that should be fair, and as he thought meet for the room".[10]

The last line of Anne Basset's letter strongly suggests that her sister was not a beauty, and the King, to whom physical appearance mattered, was reluctant to appoint her.

Or perhaps there was yet another reason for Henry's refusal. His marriage to Anne of Cleves was a failure. "I like her not!" the King famously exclaimed after seeing his future bride for the first time. Although the irritated Henry VIII tried to extricate himself from the commitment, his councillors failed

---

[9] Elizabeth Norton, *Anne of Cleves*, p. 82.
[10] Ibid., p. 83.

to find an impediment to the marriage, and the wedding took place on 6 January 1540.

When Thomas Cromwell broached the delicate subject of the wedding night with Henry VIII the next morning, the King said that he liked Anne of Cleves "much worse" after their disastrous first night together. According to Henry VIII, Anne of Cleves was not a virgin, and after he had "felt her belly and breasts . . . I had neither will nor courage to proceed any further in other matters". That same morning, Henry discussed the matter with his physicians. He found Anne unattractive and unable to "excite and provoke any lust in him". He could not, he explained, "overcome this loathsomeness, nor in her company be provoked or stirred to that act". The union was, in other words, still not consummated. The King, however, was not implying that he was impotent. He explained to his doctors that he considered himself able to "do the act" with other women because he had two "wet dreams", but it was Anne who failed to arouse desire in him.[11] Although Henry tried to consummate the marriage over the coming nights, he did not succeed.

Anne must have known that something was amiss because she "has often desired" to speak to Thomas Cromwell. Cromwell, however, dared not speak with the Queen about her

---

[11] Starkey, *Six Wives*, p. 632.

marital problems, knowing only too well that discussing the King's sexual prowess could be a sufficient ground to lost one's head (hence the example of Anne Boleyn and her brother). Instead, he instructed the Queen's English ladies-in-waiting to provoke a discussion about the intimate secrets of the royal bedchamber.

On one occasion during a hot June evening, Ladies Rochford, Rutland and Edgecombe approached the Queen and told her that they assumed she was still a virgin. How could this be, the Queen marvelled, if she slept every night with the King? Lady Rochford, herself a widow since 1536 and well versed in what was required of a married couple in bed, frankly told Anne of Cleves that "there must be more than that" to lose one's virginity. Anne of Cleves explained that apart from kissing her at night and in the morning, the King did not proceed any further. "Is this not enough?" she asked with a childlike naivety. "Madam, there must be more than this", Lady Rutland replied, "or otherwise we shall never get a Duke of York, which is what this kingdom is longing for."

Anne of Cleves's comments had been taken at face value and interpreted that she had no idea of what conjugal duties really meant. Historian Elizabeth Norton challenged this notion in her biography of Anne of Cleves, pointing out that the Queen's knowledge of the English language was scant at the time—she still needed a translator to help her make sense of what the English delegates told her in July 1540, when the King sent them to acquaint Anne with his plans of divorcing her—and that the conversation might not have occurred at all.[12]

If this is the case, then there are two possibilities. First is that Anne of Cleves might have been afraid of what would happen to her if she refused to acknowledge that her marriage was a farce—she could have been banished and sentenced to live out her days in bleak penury, like Katherine of Aragon, or face execution, like Anne Boleyn—so she decided to accept the King's terms and confess anything he wanted to hear. The second possibility is that the depositions of the English ladies-in-waiting, who related during the legal process the above-mentioned conversation with Anne of Cleves, were not entirely truthful. It would have been neither the first nor the last time ladies-in-waiting would play a major role in the undoing of a queen, providing false testimonies.

It seems highly unlikely that Anne of Cleves, who was praised for her wit and intelligence, was unaware that a marriage must be consummated in order to be deemed legal and indissoluble, much less that she would talk about the King's sexual prowess with her English ladies-in-waiting. Interestingly, Anne's confidante, Mrs Loew, was not asked to

---

[12] Elizabeth Norton, *Anne of Cleves*, p. 74.

give a deposition concerning the Queen's marital life. According to Ladies Rochford, Rutland and Edgecombe, the Queen was ashamed to speak about such intimate matters with Mrs Loew, whom she had known for a very long time. "God forbid", was her reply to Lady Rutland's question of whether she confided in Mrs Loew. Again, it seems highly unlikely that Anne of Cleves would choose to confide in the English ladies considering that she was not fluent in English and that they had been total strangers to her after a mere six months of acquaintance.

Furthermore, the Queen was genuinely surprised and upset when she learned that Henry VIII wanted to divorce her; would she have been so surprised if the conversation with her ladies-in-waiting indeed took place? It is utterly incomprehensible that Anne of Cleves could have been so ignorant of what was happening around her.

Whatever the truth behind this matter, Anne of Cleves's marriage to Henry VIII was annulled on grounds of non-consummation. Her consent earned her the King's gratefulness and financial stability. The palaces of Richmond and Bletchingley were now hers, and she was officially styled as Henry VIII's sister.

The King did not wait long to remarry because he was already in the thralls of love with the Duke of Norfolk's niece and Anne Boleyn's first cousin, Katherine Howard, who served as Anne of Cleves's maid of honour. The King was yet again in love with a girl of the Howard family, and yet again he would come to regret it.

Chapter 13:

The ladies of Katherine Howard

When Henry VIII married Katherine Howard, he was a shadow of his former self. No longer a young and athletic man, the King suffered from ulcers on his legs and was not as physically active as he used to be. Katherine Howard was a breath of fresh air: young, pretty and vivacious. The King was in love again and showed Katherine more affection than he had to any of his previous wives. The court was again filled with young women dressed in fashionable French gowns who served about the Queen.

An inventory of the torrent of gifts which the King had begun to shower on Katherine by the summer of 1540 remarkably survives to this day and reveals that Henry VIII spared no expense for elaborate trimmings to decorate Katherine's French hoods, costly necklaces studded with diamonds, rubies, pearls and emeralds, golden brooches to pin to her bodices and bejewelled girdles to wear around her waist. The anonymous author of the contemporary *Spanish Chronicle* sang praises for Katherine, asserting that she was "more graceful and beautiful than any lady in the court, or perhaps in the kingdom" and even the most beautiful of Henry VIII's wives.[1]

The same *Spanish Chronicle* suggested that Katherine was "no more than fifteen" when the King fell in love with her, but the fact that she became the Queen's maid of honour in 1540 points to the possibility that she was at least sixteen at the time, the minimum age required to receive such a post at court. It is also possible that as a niece of the leading peer and one of the most influential men at court, Katherine owed her post to Thomas Howard, Duke of Norfolk. If this is indeed the case, she may have been younger than sixteen, just as the duke's daughter was when she became Anne Boleyn's maid of honour at the age of thirteen in 1532.

However, there is a hint of evidence that Henry VIII was not drawn to very young women and had never engaged in a sexual relationship with a teenager before. His first wife was six years his senior, while Anne Boleyn was ten years younger, and Jane Seymour was twenty years younger, although both were in their mid-twenties when they caught the King's wandering eye. When Francis I's daughter was offered as Henry VIII's prospective bride in December 1537, the English King rejected the match out of hand saying that the seventeen-year-old Madeleine de Valois was "too young for

---

[1] *Chronicle of King Henry VIII of England (The Spanish Chronicle)*, pp. 75-77.

him".[2] Anne of Cleves, the King's fourth wife, was twenty-four years younger than Henry VIII at the time of their wedding, but she was entering her mid-twenties, and it was her portrait as well as her age that helped Henry select her for his bride. While popular culture often portrays Katherine Howard as an already promiscuous child bride, it is highly likely, considering the presented evidence, that she was more than sixteen years old when the King noticed her, and so, according to the standards of the era she lived in, she was no longer a child. Her exact age is, however, still a matter of conjecture among historians.

Katherine might have been presented to Henry VIII by the Duke of Norfolk, as the later rumours suggested that he was an "author of this marriage".[3] Norfolk was a survivor in the ruthless environment of the court, where vices such as pride, envy and derision were a vital part of everyday life. He was prepared to exploit Henry VIII's interest in his niece to his own advantage and was always looking for what he could gain as the Queen's uncle.

Norfolk never allowed his family ties to interfere with his loyalty to the King, however. When his Boleyn relatives fell from favour, he distanced himself from them and presided over the trials of Anne and George Boleyn as Lord High

---

[2] *Letters and Papers*, Henry VIII, Volume 12 Part 2, note 1285.
[3] *Letters and Papers*, Henry VIII, Volume 16, note 1332.

Steward. It is probably fair to say that Norfolk was a good judge of people's characters, and this attribute helped him navigate through the murky waters of courtly politics. The fact that he had foretold Anne Boleyn's downfall and managed to distance himself from her at the right moment proves that he had a very well-developed sense of self-preservation.

The fact that he was considered to be the architect of Katherine Howard's royal marriage proves effectively that he must have had a high opinion of his young niece. Norfolk had already had a niece on the throne who threatened his position and the well-being of his entire family and, had Katherine Howard been as famously unpredictable, as it is often suggested, she would have been kept away from court for fear of disgracing the Howards. This sole fact flies in the face of common opinion that Katherine was a foolish girl who blurted out secrets about her past to everyone, as has been suggested in recent fictional portrayals.

Yet the young Queen's past would come back to haunt her. Before her wedding to Henry VIII took place, Agnes Tilney, Dowager Duchess of Norfolk, in whose household Katherine spent her girlhood, was especially keen to impart her advice on how the girl should handle her royal suitor and presented her with new, fashionable clothes to enhance her appearance. Just what kind of advice Katherine Howard was given remains a mystery. One of the possibilities is that the Dowager Duchess of Norfolk, who was Katherine's step-grandmother and something of a mother figure to the orphaned girl, instructed her to put a price on her virginity, even if Katherine was no longer a virgin, as it would come to light after her wedding. Everyone at court knew that Henry VIII desired his prospective bride to be of high moral purity and a virgin. Katherine lost her virginity in the dowager duchess's household, but this fact was kept hidden from the King.

Even before Katherine Howard became Queen, her former friends started petitioning her for help. Joan Bulmer, a young girl who lived with Katherine in Agnes Tilney's household, wrote Katherine a letter professing her love and wishing her all honour and prosperity. She also implored Katherine to appoint her as one of her serving women. Katherine granted Joan's wish and appointed her as one of her chamberers.

"Light both in conditions and living"

Serving in the Queen's household was the highest of privileges for any woman who sought to build up a successful career at court, but not all young women were eager to enter

Katherine Howard's household. Mary Lascelles Hall, who shared a room with Katherine in the Dowager Duchess of Norfolk's household, where they both were raised up, did not have a high opinion of the young Queen. When Mary's brother, John Lascelles, encouraged her to exploit an opportunity and seek employment with Katherine, Mary retorted that the Queen was "light both in conditions and living".[4]

Henry VIII could hardly believe that his beloved young wife was not as chaste as he wanted her to be. Nevertheless, he ordered an investigation to clear Katherine's name from slander. In due course, it was revealed that Katherine Howard was not a virgin when she married the King. She had shared a sexual relationship with her old flame who lived in the dowager duchess's household, Francis Dereham (Katherine also employed him when she became Queen) and her music teacher, Henry Manox.

Disbanded household

Katherine Howard's conduct before she married Henry VIII was immodest, but everyone at court knew that the King could not punish Katherine for her premarital sexual experience. He could, and indeed he would, terminate his

---

[4] Ibid., note 1334.

marriage to her. The King was displeased and decided to disband Katherine's household:

"This year, the 13th day of November, Sir Thomas Wriothesley, knight, and Secretary to the King, came to Hampton Court to the Queen, and called all the ladies and gentlewomen and her servants into the Great Chamber, and there openly afore them declared certain offences that she had done in misusing her body with certain persons afore the King's time, wherefore he there discharged all her household."[5]

The next day, Katherine was taken to Syon Abbey, attended by her half sister, Lady Baynton, and three other gentlewomen of her own choice. Additionally, she was allowed to keep two chamberers. Katherine also had "a mean number of servants" to tend to her daily requirements; the French ambassador revealed that there was a dozen of them. Although still technically Queen, Katherine was no longer living in opulence. She was to dress modestly as befitted a woman in her situation. The three chambers which she occupied were hung with "mean stuff", and she was not entitled to sit or dine under a cloth of estate.[6]

---

[5] *Wriothesley's Chronicle*, Vol. 1, pp. 130-131.
[6] *State Papers, King Henry the Eighth*, Vol. 1, pp. 691-692.

With the Queen's disgrace, her remaining ladies-in-waiting found themselves out of jobs. The Privy Council's instructions for Thomas Cranmer touched upon the matter of what to do with the female servants. Some of the Queen's ladies were sent to serve Lady Mary, the King's elder daughter. Margaret Douglas, the King's niece, was to be conducted to the Duke of Norfolk's house at Kenninghall, together with Norfolk's daughter, Mary Howard. The other ladies were not forgotten either:

"Order must be also taken with the maidens, that they repair each of them to their friends, there to remain; saving Mistress Basset, whom the King's Majesty, in consideration of the calamity of her friends, will, at his charges, specially provide for. And if the number of the Queen's house, necessarily furnished in the proportion written unto you, there remain any of the Queen's servants unprovided for, whereof you think the King's Highness should have consideration, for as much as they have no home or friends to resort, or means convenient to live, we shall, upon your signification of their names, without delay, labour to know the King's Highness pleasure; to the intent the household may be dissolved, with as much contention, and reasonable satisfaction of the parties, as the nature and quality of the cause thereof doth permit and suffer."[7]

This piece of evidence shows that ladies-in-waiting and maids of honour were highly regarded by the King, who took care of them whenever any of his wives lost favour with him. Interestingly, Henry VIII graciously allowed Katherine Howard to pick three ladies to serve her at Syon Abbey, a privilege denied to Anne Boleyn when she was arrested in 1536.

Confessions

During his interrogation, Francis Dereham revealed that Thomas Culpeper, one of the Gentlemen of the King's Privy Chamber, shared an intimate relationship with Katherine Howard. Immodest behaviour before the marriage to Henry VIII was nothing in comparison to marital infidelity. Culpeper was arrested and examined. He claimed that he never committed adultery with the Queen, and it was Katherine who "pined for him, and was actually dying of love for his person".[8]

---

[7] Ibid.
[8] *Calendar of State Papers, Spain*, Volume 6 Part 1, note 209.

According to Culpeper, Katherine enlisted the help of her trusted lady-in-waiting, Jane Parker Boleyn, Lady Rochford, to arrange their meetings. Lady Rochford was already notorious for being "a widow of that nobleman [George Boleyn] who was capitally punished, as you know, for incest with his sister, Queen Anne".[9] The French ambassador Marillac was harsh in his assessment of Lady Rochford's character; she was a woman "who all her life had the name to esteem her honour little, and has thus in her old age shown little amendment."[10] We do not know what Marillac was referring to. Did he know something about Lady Rochford that is lost to us? Perhaps Lady Rochford's conduct during her husband's trial was widely known at the time. Although her involvement in the downfall of the Boleyn siblings narrowed down to a confession of a conversation she had with Anne Boleyn about the King's sexual potency, it was nevertheless a crucial piece of evidence which sent George Boleyn to the block.[11]

Perhaps we may, if we choose to, read more into Lady Rochford's advice to Katherine Howard to say nothing about her affair with Thomas Culpeper, warning the Queen that the interrogators "would speak fair to you and use all ways with

---

[9] Elizabeth Norton, *The Boleyn Women*, p. 229.
[10] *Letters and Papers*, Volume 16, note 1366.
[11] Read more in Chapter 10.

you, but if you confess you undo both yourself and others."[12] Was Lady Rochford drawing on her own experiences of the 1536 interrogation? Sadly, we may never know, but it is a tempting possibility to link her warning with what she had endured in May 1536.

Unfortunately, Katherine Howard turned against her lady-in-waiting and blamed her for everything. The young Queen maintained that "Lady Rochford hath sundry times made instance to her to speak with Culpeper, declaring him to bear her goodwill and favour".[13] Katherine's letter to Culpeper, however, reveals a different side of the story. When Culpeper fell ill, the young Queen wrote that she longed to see him, and the thought of not being around him made her heart die. She also informed Culpeper that he should come to her whenever Lady Rochford was around because only then was Katherine able to meet him. It is clearly a letter from a love-stricken teenager rather than someone who was pressured by her lady-in-waiting.

Lady Rochford certainly played a major part in Katherine Howard's affair. She allowed the young lovers to meet in her chamber on one occasion and was present during their meetings, albeit sitting "somewhat far off or turned her

---

[12] Examination of Queen Katherine Howard (*Calendar of the Manuscripts of the Marquis of Bath*, Vol. 2, p. 10)
[13] Ibid.

back".[14] Although Katherine Howard maintained that she had never committed adultery with Thomas Culpeper, Lady Rochford had a very different opinion. She believed that "Culpeper has known the Queen carnally".[15] Culpeper, for his part, shifted the blame on Lady Rochford, saying that she "provoked him much to love the Queen".[16]

The real extent of Lady Rochford's participation in this affair remains unclear despite the fact that all parties involved in it were interrogated. She was certainly aware that execution was a real possibility, especially when she learned that Dereham and Culpeper were tried and sent to the block, and, as the imperial ambassador reported, she "had been seized with a fit of madness by which her brain is affected" three days after her arrest.[17] Jane was well aware that an insane person could avoid death at the scaffold, but the King was apparently sceptical about her condition. Chapuys reported that Lady Rochford had lucid intervals, something that strongly suggests her insanity might have been feigned. Henry VIII sent his own physicians to nurse Lady Rochford back to

---

[14] Ibid.
[15] *Letters and Papers*, Volume 16, note 1339.
[16] Ibid.
[17] *Calendar of State Papers, Spain*, Volume 6 Part 1, note 209.

health because he was eager to have her executed as an example to others.[18]

In February 1542, the Act of Parliament declared that even an insane person could be executed for treason. Chapuys reported that Lady Rochford had recovered her senses at "the very moment" she learned that she must die.[19] Katherine Howard and Lady Rochford were executed on 13 February 1542. The young Queen's fate was a grim lesson to any lady who was courted by Henry VIII. Indeed, as the imperial ambassador remarked, "there are few, if any, ladies at court nowadays likely to aspire to the honour of becoming one of the King's wives".[20] The women who served about Henry VIII's wives knew all too well that being married to the King was not always a privilege. Although the crown was within reach of ladies-in-waiting, even the crowned heads of Henry VIII's bedfellows could roll.

---

[18] Ibid.

[19] Ibid.

[20] Ibid., note 232.

Chapter 14:

The end of the reign: Katherine Parr's servants

Henry VIII's sixth wife was Katherine Parr. She was well-educated, pious and a kind woman of thirty-two. She took it upon herself to bring the royal family back together and thrived in her role as stepmother to Henry VIII's three children. Ladies Mary and Elizabeth, as well as Prince Edward, enjoyed Katherine's company and recognised that she introduced an element of stability to their family life. The King was fond enough of Katherine to appoint her as regent during his war campaign in France in 1544.

Changes in the Queen's household

Despite the rapid succession of wives between 1536 and 1543, there was a continuity of staff within the household of Henry VIII's queens. But when Katherine Parr became Queen in 1543, certain changes occurred in the new household. After her husband's death in 1543, the Countess of Rutland—who was a dominant force in the establishments of

Henry VIII's previous wives—retired from court and was replaced by Katherine Parr's sister, Anne Parr Herbert. Apart from her sister, with whom she shared a close relationship, Katherine Parr employed three other kinswomen as ladies-in-waiting: Elizabeth Tyrwhitt, Maud Parr Lane and Mary Parr were newcomers to court.

The most important link between Katherine Parr and her ladies-in-waiting was their faith. By 1543, the New Religion had already gained a steady number of followers, and Katherine Parr was one of them. She wrote two devotional books, held Bible studies in her chambers and enjoyed discussing religious matters with Henry VIII and her ladies. Four of the most prominent ladies-in-waiting in the Queen's Privy Chamber were well-grounded in the new teachings and shared very close relationships with Katherine Parr; Anne Parr Herbert, the Queen's own sister; Katherine Willoughby Brandon, Duchess of Suffolk; Anne Stanhope Seymour, now Countess of Hertford and Elizabeth Oxenbridge Tyrwhitt.

Katherine Willoughby, Duchess of Suffolk, was the daughter of Katherine of Aragon's principal lady-in-waiting and lifelong friend, Maria de Salinas. Katherine's father, Lord William Willoughby de Eresby, died in 1526, and two years later, young Katherine became the ward of Charles Brandon, Duke of Suffolk. The duke planned to marry Katherine to his son, the Earl of Lincoln. Brandon's wife, Mary Tudor (sister of

Henry VIII), died in June 1533, and the Duke decided to marry Katherine Willoughby himself. She was only fourteen at that time, while Brandon was approaching his fiftieth birthday.

The wedding ceremony took place on 7 September 1533. Katherine Willoughby became the Duchess of Suffolk and one of the most prominent ladies of the court since her husband was Henry VIII's close friend and servant. The couple had two sons: Henry, born in 1535, and Charles, born two years later. Charles Brandon died in 1545, leaving Katherine a widow. Katherine Willoughby shared a close relationship with Katherine Parr. They both lost their fathers at a young age and both were raised by their mothers. Also, their mothers had long-standing ties to Katherine of Aragon, who stood as godmother to both Katherine Parr and Katherine Willoughby.

In 1546, an attempt was made to associate the evangelical circle at court with Anne Askew, who was deemed a heretic and burned in the summer of that year. The conservative faction, led by Bishop Stephen Gardiner, used Anne Askew's arrest to implicate Katherine Parr and her ladies. It was also hoped that through the ladies of the court, their prominent husbands would be implicated, and the court would be purged from so called heretics. Had the plot worked, the Catholic conservatives would have controlled access to

Henry VIII, whose health was rapidly deteriorating, and secured their grip on Prince Edward's regency council.

Katherine Willoughby, who had a dog named Gardiner, after the bishop whom she loathed, was among the targeted women. Anne Askew was pressured during the interrogation—she had been cruelly tortured—to implicate Katherine Willoughby, Anne Seymour and Joan Denny, but Askew confessed nothing except the fact that servants of Ladies Denny and Seymour sent her some money to sustain herself.

Both Anne Stanhope Seymour and Joan Champernowne Denny were wives of leading courtiers. Edward Seymour and Anthony Denny were prominent Reformers and stood high in the King's favour. Katherine Willoughby, on the other hand, was the widow of Henry VIII's friend, and some rumours were circulating that he considered taking her as his seventh wife.[1]

In the end, however, neither the Queen nor any of her ladies were arrested as heretics. The King was not in a mood to execute yet another wife, and he turned his wrath to those who dared to attack Katherine Parr and her circle. The

---

[1] Historian Robert Hutchinson believes that rumours of Henry VIII's remarriage formed part of a "whispering campaign against Henry's consort". (Hutchinson, *The Last Days of Henry VIII*, p. 166)

conservative faction's attempt to eliminate Henry's wife and his closest servants—people whose company he enjoyed and whom he liked on a personal level—turned out to be a poor choice indeed. Two of the targeted men, Edward Seymour and Anthony Denny, were appointed as executors of Henry VIII's will and given £500 and £300 respectively.[2] This shows just how much the King trusted them.

After Henry

After the King's death in January 1547, Katherine Parr hastily remarried. Her new husband, Thomas Seymour (Queen Jane's younger brother), had been chosen by her before Henry VIII decided to marry Katherine. The Queen Dowager's new marriage, however, caused outrage at court. She remarried in a matter of months after Henry VIII's death and failed to consult the nine-year-old King Edward VI or the Lord Protector, Edward Seymour. The new marriage changed Katherine Parr's social position. While she had been presiding over the court as Henry VIII's wife and became the Queen Dowager after his death, by marrying the Lord Protector's younger brother, she became Lady Seymour.

---

[2] B.L., Harleian MS 293, fols. 111, 112, 113v.

Some sources, including the notoriously unreliable *Spanish Chronicle*, claimed that Edward Seymour's wife, who served as Katherine's lady-in-waiting in the past and who now enjoyed the title of Duchess of Somerset, was quick to point out that Katherine Parr no longer had the right to be treated as Queen. According to *The Spanish Chronicle* and later works using it as a source of information, the two women fought for precedence at court. While it is an undeniable fact that the Seymour brothers rivalled each other and their wives disliked one another as well, there is no evidence that Katherine Parr and Anne Stanhope Seymour quarrelled about which one of them was more important. Their quarrel might have been based on the subject of Katherine Parr's queenly jewels and dower lands, confiscated by the Lord Protector.

The court of Edward VI, who was only a child when he became King, was not the best place for women who sought employment as ladies-in-waiting. There was no queen to serve, and the only alternative was to seek employment in the households of Katherine Parr, Ladies Mary and Elizabeth or other ladies of high social standing, such as duchesses or countesses.

This situation changed in 1553 and 1558, when Henry VIII's daughters, Mary and Elizabeth, became Queen respectively. Both queens surrounded themselves with women who stayed loyal to them over the years and revolutionised the post of lady-in-waiting. Women were now much more influential than under Henry VIII's reign because men were excluded from the Queen's Privy Chamber, and they had to rely on ladies-in-waiting who tended to Mary and Elizabeth to obtain favours for their male counterparts. Ladies-in-waiting were never as important as under the reigns of Mary and Elizabeth, but that is another story to tell . . .

Epilogue

Ever since its beginnings, the royal court was very much a male-dominated assembly, but by the 1290s, when the household of the Queen consort became an important unit in its own right, the position of women started slowly gaining importance. The post of a lady-in-waiting emerged from relative obscurity during the reign of King Edward III, who strove to create a magnificent court modelled on the ancient Camelot. Whereas previous Queens consort kept a small number of ladies-in-waiting, Edward III's wife, Philippa of Hainault, surrounded herself with large numbers of noblewomen: in this way, her own status and magnificence were emphasised. It was during Edward III's reign that the first lady-in-waiting came to be noticed by chroniclers. Alice Perrers became the King's mistress, yet she never succeeded in becoming his wife.

It was during the reign of Henry VIII that a lady-in-waiting became a Queen. The term "in waiting" meant more or less "in attendance" and implied a role in the backdrop of courtly life. The meteoric rise of Anne Boleyn showed, however, that a Queen's serving woman could step out of obscurity and become Queen herself, but it also carried a grim warning. Anne Boleyn and three of her English successors relied solely on Henry VIII's affection to shield them from the whirlwind of political intrigues, whereas foreign royal-born brides relied on their powerful relatives. Henry VIII admitted that he preferred being married to one of his female subjects because he could punish and get rid of her whenever she misbehaved. Becoming Queen was the highest of privileges a Tudor lady-in-waiting could aspire to, but it was also one of the most dangerous positions she could attain.

Ladies-in-waiting were not mere ornaments of the court who accompanied Henry VIII's Queens on occasions of state, although, as Francis I once famously remarked, "a court without ladies was like a garden without flowers". Ladies-in-waiting also formed part of royal consorts' daily lives and often became their confidantes. One of the most desired perquisites of ladies-in-waiting was their influence in gaining posts, pensions and lands for their family and dense network of friends and clients. Henry VIII, a natural showman, thrived in the company of the ladies who served at court and often banqueted with them. The notion of courtly love put maids of honour and ladies-in-waiting in the centre of chivalric pursuits, making their presence at court an important element of everyday life. Dances, banquets, pageants, masks, tournaments and hunts formed an integral part of life at the magnificent court of Henry VIII. Women were not only expected to take part in such activities but to excel in them.

Although the Tudor court produced many fascinating women who started their brilliant careers as ladies-in-waiting, hitherto, no study has been made of the role of a lady-in-waiting at the court of Henry VIII. The women who served in the courts of Tudor Queens Mary and Elizabeth attracted much scholarly attention, but the roles of ladies-in-waiting who served Henry VIII's six wives were, until now, very much unknown territory. Yet it is impossible to study the court of Henry VIII without appreciating the achievements of ladies-in-waiting. Functions and duties generally performed by ladies-in-waiting included proficiency in foreign languages, embroidery, music making, horseback riding, hunting and other activities to pass the time with the Queen. Experienced ladies often supervised servants in the Queen's household, took care of royal clothes and jewels, relayed private messages upon command and kept their royal mistress well-informed about goings-on at court. Maids of honour, on the other hand, were young and unmarried girls expected to learn their duties from ladies-in-waiting. A suitable marriage was deemed necessary to forward their careers from maids of honour to ladies-in-waiting. These female servants were highly valued members of the royal household who developed close relationships not only with Henry VIII's Queens but also with each other. They were aristocratic, highly cultured and talented members of the royal establishment.

Selected Bibliography

Primary sources

Burnet, G. *Bishop Burnet's History of the Reformation of the Church of England, Volume 1.* R. Priestley, 1820.

Calendar of State Papers, Spain (1862-1932)

Cavendish, G. *The Life and Death of Cardinal Wolsey.* S.W. Singer, Harding and Leppard, ed. 1827.

Clifford, H. *The Life of Jane Dormer, Duchess of Feria.* Burns & Oates, 1887.

Giustiniani, S. *Four Years at the Court of Henry VIII. Two Volumes.* London, Smith, Elder, 1854, tr. Rawdon Brown.

Letters and Papers, Foreign and Domestic, of the Reign of Henry VIII (1862-1932)

The Lisle Letters, ed. Muriel St Clare Byrne. Six Volumes. The University of Chicago Press, 1981.

William Latymer's Cronickille of Anne Bulleyne, ed. Maria Dowling, Camden Miscellany, xxx (Camden Soc. 4th ser. 39, 1990).

Secondary sources

Bernard, G.W. *Anne Boleyn: Fatal Attractions.* Yale University Press, 2010.

Boland, B., St. Clare, M. *The Lisle Letters: An Abridgement.* University of Chicago Press, 1983.

Bruce, M.L. *Anne Boleyn.* Putnam Pub Group, 1972.

Childs, J. *Henry VIII's Last Victim: The Life and Times of Henry Howard, Earl of Surrey.* Thomas Dunne Books, 2007.

Denny, J. *Anne Boleyn: A New Life of England's Tragic Queen.*

Piatkus Books Ltd., 2005.

Everett Wood, A. *Letters of Royal and Illustrious Ladies of Great Britain. Three Volumes.* London, H. Colburn, 1846.

Friedmann, P. *Anne Boleyn: A Chapter of English History, 1527-1536.* Macmillan and Co., 1884.

Furdel Lane, E. *The Royal Doctors, 1485-1714: Medical Personnel at the Tudor and Stuart Courts.* University of Rochester Press, 2001.

Gladish, Dorothy M. *The Tudor Privy Council.* Redford, 1915.

Harkrider, F.M. *Women, Reform and Community in Early Modern England.* Boydell Press, 2008.

Harris, B. *Marriage Sixteenth-Century Style: Elizabeth Stafford and the Third Duke of Norfolk.* Journal of Social History, Vol. 15, No. 3, Special Issue on the History of Love (Spring 1982), pp. 371-382.

Harris, J. B. *English Aristocratic Women, 1450-1550 : Marriage and Family, Property and Careers.* Oxford University Press, 2002.
The View from My Lady's Chamber: New Perspectives on the Early Tudor Monarchy. Huntington Library Quarterly, Vol. 60, No. 3, The Remapping of English Political History, 1500-1640 (1997), pp. 215-247.

Harris, N. *Testamenta Vetusta. Two Volumes.* Nicholas & Son, 1826.

Haynes, S. *A Collection of State Papers.*

Head, M. D. *The Ebbs and Flows of Fortune: The Life of Thomas Howard, Third Duke of Norfolk.* University of Georgia Press, 1995.

Hibbert, C. *The Virgin Queen: A Personal History of Elizabeth I.* Tauris Parke Paperbacks, 2010.

Hutchinson, R. *The Last Days of Henry VIII: Conspiracy, Treason and Heresy at the Court of the Dying Tyrant.* Phoenix, 2006.

Ives, E. W. *The Life and Death of Anne Boleyn: The Most Happy.* Blackwell Publishing, 2010.

Lipscomb, S. *1536: The Year that Changed Henry VIII.* Lion Hudson, 2009.

Norton, E. *Anne of Cleves: Henry VIII's Discarded Bride.* Amberley Publishing,

2011.

Bessie Blount: Mistress to Henry VIII. Amberley Publishing, 2012.

Jane Seymour: Henry VIII's True Love. Amberley Publishing, 2010.

The Boleyn Women: The Tudor Femmes Fatales Who Changed English History. Amberley Publishing, 2013.

Orme, N. *From Childhood to Chivalry: The Education of the English Kings and Aristocracy, 1066-1530.* Taylor & Francis, 1984.

Porter, L. *Katherine the Queen: The Remarkable Life of Katherine Parr.* Macmillan, 2010.

Scarisbrick, J.J. *Henry VIII.* University of California Press, 1968.

Shulman, N. *Graven with Diamonds.* Short Books, 2011.

Smith, Lacey B. *Catherine Howard: The Queen Whose Adulteries Made a Fool of Henry VIII.* Amberley Publishing, 2009.

Somerset, A. *Ladies-in-Waiting: From the Tudors to the Present Day.* Phoenix, 2005.

Starkey, D. *Elizabeth: The Struggle for the Throne.* Harper Perennial, 2007.

Starkey, D. *Six Wives: The Queens of Henry VIII.* Vintage, 2004.

Tremlett, G. *Catherine of Aragon: Henry's Spanish Queen.* Faber & Faber, 2010.

Walker, G. *Rethinking the Fall of Anne Boleyn.* The Historical Journal, Vol. 45, No. 1 (Mar., 2002), pp. 1-29.

Warnicke, R.M. *The Rise and Fall of Anne Boleyn: Family Politics at the Court of Henry VIII.* Cambridge University Press, 1991.

Weir, A. *Mary Boleyn: 'The Great and Infamous Whore'.* Vintage, 2011.

The Lady in the Tower: The Fall of Anne Boleyn. Vintage, 2010.

The Six Wives of Henry VIII. Vintage, 2007.

Whitelock, A. *Mary Tudor: England's First Queen.* Bloomsbury Publishing, 2010.

Williams, P. *Catherine of Aragon: The Tragic Story of Henry VIII's First Unfortunate Wife.* Amberley Publishing, 2013.

Wilson, A. V. *Queen Elizabeth's Maids of Honour and Ladies of the Privy*

Chamber. John Lane, 1922.

Unpublished PhD Thesis

Merton, Ch.I. *The Women who served Queen Mary and Queen Elizabeth: Ladies, Gentlewomen and Maids of the Privy Chamber, 1553 – 1603.* University of Cambridge, 1991.

Websites

http://www.british-history.ac.uk
http://www.juliafox.co.uk
www.archive.org